LIVING WITH AMBIGUITY

living with

Discerning God in a Complex Society

ambiguity

donald j.
foran, sj

alba house   alba house   DIVISION OF THE SOCIETY OF ST. PAUL
STATEN ISLAND, N.Y. 10314

Imprimi Potest
    John J. Kelley, S.J., Prov.

Nihil Obstat
    Daniel V. Flynn, J.C.D.
    Censor Librorum

Imprimatur
    Joseph P. O'Brien, S.T.D.
    Vicar General, Archdiocese of New York
    June 19, 1970

The nihil obstat and imprimatur are official declarations that a book or pamphlet is free of doctrinal or moral error. No implication is contained therein that those who have granted the nihil obstat and imprimatur agree with the contents, opinions or statements expressed.

Library of Congress Catalog Card Number: 72-140282

SBN: 8189-0196-9

Designed, printed and bound in the U.S.A. by the Pauline Fathers and Brothers of the Society of St. Paul, 2187 Victory Blvd., Staten Island, N.Y. 10314 as part of their communications apostolate.

To my parents
To the Jesuit Order
To many families and friends:
This book is the least that I owe you.

ACKNOWLEDGEMENTS

"A Coney Island of the Mind, #25," Lawrence Ferlinghetti, **a Coney Island of the Mind.** Copyright © 1958 by Lawrence Ferlinghetti. Reprinted by permission of New Directions Publishing Corporation.

"A Prayer for My Daughter," reprinted with permission of the Macmillan Company, 1952 by Bertha Georgie Yeats from **Collected Poems** by William Butler Yeats. Copyright © 1924 by The Macmillan Company renewed 1952 by Bertha Georgie Yeats.

"The Choice," reprinted with permission of The Macmillan Company from **Collected Poems** by William Butler Yeats. Copyright © 1933 by The Macmillan Company, renewed 1961 by Bertha Georgie Yeats. Both poems also authorized by Mr. M.B. Yeats and the Macmillan Companies of London and Canada.

"Prayer on the Six P.M. Subway," reprinted with permission of The Macmillan Company from **Love, Love at the End** by Daniel Berrigan, S.J., Copyright © by Daniel Berrigan, S.J., 1966.

"Georgy Girl," copyright 1966 by Springfield Music, Ltd. Chappell & Co., Inc., Used by permission Chappell Co., Inc.

Scarlet Ribbons by Evelyn Danzig and Jack Segal. Copyright © 1949 by Mills Music, Inc.

The Persecution and Assassination of Jean-Paul Marat as Performed by the Inmates of the Asylum of Charenton under the Direction of the Marquis de Sade by Peter Weiss. English version by Geoffrey Skelton, verse adaptation by Adrian Mitchell. Copyright © 1965 by John Calder Ltd. Reprinted by permission of Atheneum Publishers.

A New Catechism: Catholic Faith for Adults, published by Herder & Herder, 232 Madison Avenue, New York, N.Y. 10016.

·

TABLE OF CONTENTS

Not knowing how to find the open air,
But toiling desperately to find it out . . .
Torment myself."

Richard in Henry VI, Part
III. William Shakespeare

IV. Patience: "He disliked bars and bodegas. A
clean, well-lighted cafe was a very different
thing. Now, without thinking further, he
would go home to his room. He would lie in
bed, and finally, with daylight, he would
go to sleep. After all, he said to himself, it
is probably only insomnia. Many must
have it."

A waiter in Hemingway's "A
Clean, Well-Lighted Place."

V. Kindness: Linus (to Snoopy). "In regard to 'be
kind to animals week,' I have a question . . .
you animals expect to be treated a little bit
nicer by people this week . . . right? Well,
does this mean that you, in turn, are also
going to make an extra effort to be more
kind to that cat who lives next door?"

Snoopy (lying deep in thought and flat
on his back upon his doghouse roof): "I
hate questions like that."

Peanuts, created by Charles
Schulz; United Feature Syndi-
cate, May 8, 1969.

VI. Goodness: She said, "Will he be tried? It'll   77
kill his mother." So he said to her gravely,
"I tried him." Then she considered that a
long time before she said, "You forgave
him." "Yes."

From Too Late the Phalarope.
Alan Paton

VII. Fidelity: "Faith consecrates the world. Fidelity   89
communicates with it."

Teilhard de Chardin in The
Divine Milieu

VIII. Gentleness: "Meanwhile   103
Watch the indolent butterfly playing on the

tall flower in the yard
And think about the sun's going down
It always does you know."

Rod McKuen *in* Listen to
the Warm

IX. Self-Control: "And this is my prayer, that your
love may grow richer and richer in knowledge and insight of every kind and may
teach you by experience what things are
most worthwhile."

Philippians 1:9

X. Conclusions: "Be not too hasty," said Imlac, "to
trust or to admire the teachers of morality;
they discourse like angels, but they live like
men."

Samuel Johnson, in The History of Rasselas.

But the harvest of the Spirit is love, joy, peace, patience, kindness, goodness, fidelity, gentleness and self-control. There is no law dealing with such as these.

Galatians 5:22-23

INTRODUCTION

"Simon, Simon... I have prayed that your faith may not fail; and when you have come to yourself, you must lend strength to your brothers." (Luke 22:31)

"I am moved by fancies that are curled
Around these images and cling:
The notion of some infinitely gentle,
Infinitely suffering thing." (T. S. Eliot in "Preludes")

"The hardest thing in the world to do is to write straight, honest prose about human beings." Hemingway was right. The human person is much too complex an entity to nail down in print. The best writers of our own or any other time are those who present us with the protean image of a radically indefinable person. If that person lives for us; if he is real enough for us to glimpse in him the "ungraspable phantom of life" which Ishmael, Holden Caulfield, Raskolnikov, Stephen Dedalus, Santiago, and the young Prince of Denmark tried to cope with, then we usually come to realize that the "ungraspable" must remain ungraspable, and "life" must be lived, not compartmentalized.

Most of us find it very easy to hurl an epithet or fashion a label. We like to smoothe out wrinkles, sand down rough edges, simplify the mysteries that are threatening precisely because they defy categorization. There is certainly enough confusion in our lives, we reason. Shouldn't it facilitate our day to day living if we are clear on what is good or bad, who is left or right, what is profound or drivel? The fact is that those who have attempted to nail down or write off mystery end up "undone" by the very pride which led them to play God in the first place. Captain Ahab tried to heap upon the white whale's back "the sum of all the general rage and hate felt by his whole race from Adam down," and make all of that confusion "practically assailable" by putting a harpoon into the whale. Raskolnikov did fundamentally the same thing to the woman pawnbroker whom he murdered with an axe. And the Pharisees did not rest until they had nailed an upstart dissenter to a tree.

Those who are uncomfortable with ambiguity, those who must dichotomize reality, rarely appreciate the complexity of humanness. The world cries out for men of discernment, for prayerful Christians who respond to the unique persons who manifest need. If that response is made by a man emancipated from his tendencies to formulate pat answers, and attached enough to one in need, then help can be rendered in a personal manner. Genuinely Christian response will never be programmed.

Our day and age more than any other requires men of discernment. Because options and possibilities proliferate in an era of mass-transit, multi-media transmission, and social iconoclasm, it is increasingly difficult to make choices which "build up the body of Christ" by constructively bettering the world. A discerning Ishmael learned to see reality "with an equal eye." Holden Caulfield gave some signs of maturing, of learning to accept reality as it is. Raskolnikov, transformed finally by Sonia's love for him, was "gradually renewed," and passed "his initiation into a new, unknown life." Santiago, the old man who wished to catch the "truly great fish," realized that he "went out too far" to get it, and that the boy Manolin's love for him was a greater value. Hamlet "thus benetted round with villainies," brooded so greatly that his inaction forced him to shoot his "arrow o'er the house," to help nobody, and to waste his potential.

Christ was discerning enough to show Simon Peter that failure can produce new strength, a necessary strength upon which others might steady themselves. The poet Eliot was discerning enough to look at tawdry urban existence and see "infinitely gentle, infinitely suffering" human beings caught in the fragmented life of the city streets. Recognizing potentially productive and happy persons tangled in the manmade webs of circumstance is the first step toward helping them exercise their human option to escape those webs.

It is the thesis of this book that awareness, discernment, compassion, and active love are the only reasonable stages in cutting through abstractions like "possibility," and in creatively concretizing possibilities in the lives of others.

The day to day incarnating of Christ in unique situations

is really the task of the reflective Christian. It is not so much a case of "constructing" Christ in order to console and be consoled. It is rather discerning Christ wherever his Spirit moves. The Spirit manifests himself in numerous ways. He is available to be confronted in the lives of all persons. And the attitude of openness to his varied presences is an attitude of prayer.

And so, the process of exercising an active compassion for the needs of others, of being a discerner in the sense of catalyzing others' discovery of options, produces a by-product of tremendous value to the one thus compassionating: he finds that he inevitably feels the need for someone or something beyond himself. Whether or not he consciously reflects on what is happening, he finds himself practicing a form of active contemplation of life's possibilities, revealed moment by moment by the God who sustains a universe fraught with options. The perceptive person's posture toward the meaningful universe is not unlike the posture of genuine prayer. It is the purpose of this book to examine the working out of discernment by responding to the concrete manifestations of the Spirit of Christ.

When we concretize possibilities in the lives of others we confront our own inadequacy; we realize our radical incapacity to broaden another's vistas alone and unaided. We know what we can do, and are realistic enough to know what we cannot.

Once we confront our own felt need for a wisdom and strength beyond our own, we are beginning to pray, beginning to affirm God's power to work through us for others.

There are obviously many people who either never have had faith in God or who for some reason have given it up, and many too who could not care less about going out to others. I am not trying to offer a panacea which will transform the lives of all who care to try the prescription. I wish, rather, to discuss with others who find themselves yearning to unlock doors, a few options open to us, particularly in those moments when our weakness clouds our sense of wonder.

Prayer, I believe, can only be defined according to context. In other words, it is a reflection upon this or that aspect of life made with an awareness of God's loving presence to it and to oneself. T. S. Eliot[1] speaks of "the apprehension of the intersection of the timeless with time" which is "the occupation of the saint." I am convinced that what he tells us are "hints and guesses, hints followed by guesses," point to a profound reality. I would formulate it thus: However the Word of God manifests itself at a particular moment of your life or of mine — whether through persons who bring you to an awareness of God's presence, or through Scripture, or through Nature; by vocalization or by meaningful silence — an Incarnation takes place, the Word becomes flesh, becomes embodied, in your life or in mine. The Timeless, God, and time, reality, intersect. I have said that prayer is defined

---

1. T. S. Eliot, "The Dry Salvages," in **Four Quartets** (New York: Harcourt, Brace and World, Inc., 1943) p. 27

according to context. If, then, my apprehension of a child's innocence and sense of wonder bring me somehow closer in my personal relationship to God, I have in effect offered a prayer of acknowledgment, lived my faith in God. The complete context of Eliot's intuition will be quoted when we are able to draw some conclusions about the depth of its meaning for us.

When I speak of faith and prayer I am enumerating graces, and every grace is a gift. In all of this, the graces that we receive — all the advents of Christ in our lives — are essentially communicable; that is, they are for our sake, and for the sake of others to whom we should impart the spirit of Christ. St. Paul says so well that God comforts us in all our troubles, so that we in turn may be able to comfort others in any trouble of theirs, and to share with them the consolation we ourselves receive from God (2 Cor. 1:4). Note that the words from St. Luke's Gospel which precede this introduction affirm the same reality.

This book is an attempt to concentrate upon nine major manifestations of God's presence to His world, His presence to each of us as unique co-creators of one another's destinies. An awareness of that presence can't help but open more of life's possibilities to us, and help us to open them to others.

In order to give the book a structural unity, I have chosen to order it around the nine manifestations of the Spirit as recorded in Galatians; in every case translating the spiritual reality into terms easily understood and appreciated by contemporary man. The nine major chapters of the book have been divided into several sub-sections. After the initial treatment of one or other of the manifestations of the Spirit, I will consider that grace as it is embodied in one's attitude toward one's self; in one's specific relationship to others; and finally, as it should be embodied in the international milieu. The final chapter will relate each of the graces examined to the premise that action on behalf of another will lead to a personal confrontation with the need for a prayerful posture toward God, and, subsequently, to a revitalized faith in the God of possibilities.

This approach should help us to avoid the tendency to turn in upon ourselves when we have failed to do what we thought we could. Self-hatred is diametrically opposed to a sound growth toward God. The prophet Jeremiah puts these words in God's mouth: "Two evils have my people done: they have forsaken me, the source of living waters; they have dug themselves cisterns, broken cisterns that hold no water" (Jer. 2:13). This solipsism is a sorry substitute for what might have been a vibrant, fulfilling partnership with God Who can be discerned working out His love in the world. The poet Hopkins shouts:

Christ plays in ten thousand places,
Lovely in limbs, and lovely in eyes not his
To the Father through the features of men's faces.[2]

---

2 Gerard Manley Hopkins, S.J., "As Kingfishers catch fire, dragon-flies draw flame," in **Poems of Gerald Manley Hopkins** (London: Oxford University Press, 1930) p. 53

Granted the seeming absence of God in the face of the world's cruelty and suffering, the discerning man or woman, the person alive to an infinity of options, will find Him in sadness and in joy. Receptivity is more active than passive. God often speaks with a very soft voice, and sometimes, not at all. He is an excellent patomimist. He communicates so much while saying so little.

CHAPTER I

LOVE

"All of us are somehow responsible to everyone for everything." —Dostoevsky

These words of the Russian novelist express, I believe, a truth as profound as the mystery of human existence itself. Love, whether it be intimate friendship or more general but nonetheless real Christian charity, extends to every human being, beginning with oneself.

A number of fresh insights characterize every new generation. Today Marshall McLuhan's hypotheses are being accepted or rejected by many. Few of us are indifferent to the things that really touch our lives. If technological developments and mass media really represent "extensions" of man, we would do well to examine the direction in which our modern media are carrying us.[1] If Teilhard de Chardin's wonderful vision is sound, if "the sacramental action of Christ, *precisely because it sanctifies matter,* extends its in-

---

1. Marshall McLuhan, **Understanding Media: The Extensions of Man** (New York: McGraw Hill Book Company, 1964) 359 pp.

fluence beyond the purely supernatural, over all that makes up the internal and external ambience of the faithful."[2] then we must react to our world, to its largeness and its beauty, as we would to any consecrated object, however externally defective. If Dostoevsky was right, if we are not only neighbors to one another, but co-creators of one anothers' destinies, then we must respond to others who, by their responses to what we are or what we ought to be, have formed us.

The crux of the matter is this: we, you and I, owe ourselves to the world; not in a vague mysterious way, but in a concrete and obvious way. When we aid one in danger of physical or spiritual death, we save ourselves. If this means risk, or as Ross Snyder defines it, "the courage to invest one's life, rather than the need to prove one's courage,"[3] let's be willing to make that investment. Risk is so much a part of true love that it is difficult to view "safe" relationships without wanting to shout out: "Be vulnerable, drop your masks, deserve to be loved and respected for who you are." Hamlet was right when he said "Conscience doth make cowards of us all" (*Hamlet*: III, i, 83). I am not suggesting that we ignore our consciences, but that we so form those consciences that genuine love be a value, not a pose; a reality, not a dream.

---

2. Pierre Teilhard de Chardin, **The Divine Milieu** (New York: Harper and Row Publishers, Harper Torchbook Edition, 1965) p. 114

3. Ross Snyder, **On Becoming Human** (Nashville, Tennessee: Abingdon Press, 1967) p. 38

Love is beautifully expressed by Holden Caulfield in Salinger's *The Catcher in the Rye*. Holden realizes what his little sister means to him, and he doesn't mind standing in the rain while he reflects upon that reality:

> Boy, it began to rain like a bastard. In *buckets*, I swear to God. All the parents and mothers and everybody went over and stood right under the roof of the carrousel, so they wouldn't get soaked to the skin or anything, but I stuck around on the bench for quite a while. I got pretty soaking wet, especially my neck and my pants. . . . I didn't care though. I felt so damn happy all of a sudden, the way old Phoebe kept going around and around, in her blue coat and all. God, I wish you could've been there.[4]

The uncritical posture in Holden is particularly refreshing because he so often seems to downgrade so much. It is not so much that he hates the things he encounters as that he fails to love himself enough to release the deep yearnings he has to love and to be loved.

After a long and bitter struggle, Bernanos' famous country priest, recognized the fact that it is "so very easy to hate ourselves." Until we accept the value that is in each of us, until we realize the potential for loving that is in us, we can-

---

4. J. D. Salinger, **The Catcher in the Rye** (Boston: Little, Brown and Company, 1951; New York: Batam Books, Inc., 1964) p. 212

not really love others effectively. Once we place ourselves before God and before men *as we are,* as a friend before a friend, faults and all, we can begin to *be* for them.

Even sporadic contact with those who are suffering — with the diseased, the perverted, the deranged, the depraved, those blacker than we, or poorer than we, or less intelligent than we — will convince the man or woman who adheres to self-value and cares for the value of others that he or she should give of himself or herself. When I admit to myself that I am radically responsible to fellow human beings, I find it a little easier to acknowledge that I am a bit human myself. Maybe we have to experience another's situation in order to appreciate our own. I have always been struck by those haunting words: "I wept because I had no shoes, and then I met a man who had no feet" (*Anon*).

You and I will meet many people who prefer to wallow in their suffering rather than preserve their human dignity. These unfortunates may be the products of countless thoughtless acts or words from persons who couldn't find time to lighten the load of one oppressed. A smile or lip-service does something when all is desolation or isolation, but is that all we have to give? How serious was Christ when he graphically painted the portrait of the real lover, he who fed the hungry, gave drink to the thirsty, clothed the naked? The hungry, thirsty, naked man was and *is* Himself. Bearing one anothers' burdens is one of the more demanding aspects of Christian love.

Sure, we all need to love and be loved, but how proportionate are our efforts to satisfy the latter and effect the former? Is there any reality to the words "community of man" and "brotherhood of nations"? And whose fault is it if there is not? Are we fundamentally affirming the status of man as Mr. Compson in Faulkner's *The Sound and the Fury* sees him: "conceived by accident and whose every breath is a freak cast with dice already loaded against him"?[5] Every Biafra presupposes a Nigeria, but neither situation is necessarily causal.

Do we love ourselves enough to break down the barriers which keep us from expressing ourselves to our world? Do we believe that in Christ we have sufficient strength to *be* Christ to ourselves and to others? Do we love others enough to receive Christ in them, and to *want* to receive him? Love, paradoxically, means "otherness" and "oneness." St. Augustine may have grasped the mystery of love between persons when he exclaimed: "There shall be one Christ loving himself."

If all of this seems too abstract, too mystical to be relevant here and now, visit a prison, a mental hospital, retirement home, or a nearby street corner. In the eyes of those who live a minimal human existence, in the eyes of those for whom life holds out no mystery and love has ceased to have a mean-

---

5. William Faulkner, **The Sound and the Fury** (New York: Vintage Books, Alfred A. Knopf, Inc. and Random House, Inc., 1946) p. 220

ing, in these thousands of eyes lies a plea: "Be a brother to me, and I will *be* just a bit longer." A woman in a state mental hospital once told me that she was in hell and had to tell someone before she lost contact with the world of other people. A man who had twice attempted suicide said that his wife was dead, his children married and he "never had any friends anyway." There is little that we can do in the face of such isolation but to offer ourselves in some small but concrete way as caring, interested persons. Sometimes nothing can be done to alleviate the suffering; but interest is a subtle affirmation of self-value to one who has given up.

A theme of the popular movie, *Georgy Girl*, urges Georgy to "bring out all the love you hide." It concludes, "What a change there'd be; the world would see a new Georgy girl." A better statement of the case might be, it seems to me: "What a change there'd be; all men would see not a new Georgy but the real Georgy, and a new world."[6]

When we see ourselves in a mirror how many of us love ourselves enough to acknowledge, "I like you?" If we dislike ourselves or are indifferent toward ourselves, something is wrong. We have failed ourselves in some way. I might add that it is possible that others have failed us too. We become, I feel, pretty much what people expect us to be. If people expect me to be a good priest, and you to be a good father or mother, then we will probably be what we are expected to be.

6. Georgy Girl: Copyright by Springfield Music, Ltd. Chappell & Company, Inc. Used by permission of Chappell Co. Inc.

Of course, we also have to expect something of ourselves.

The fact that we are not someone else, someone who really seems lovable to us, should not be discouraging: God in his wisdom saw fit to create *us;* can't we accept that? Variety is much more than the spice of life, variety is life. Nothing is more disappointing than a stereotype. Gerard Manley Hopkins penned a beautiful sonnet in praise of variation or, more specifically, in praise of the Father of all things in their ennobling differentiation. He begins,

> Glory be to God for dappled things—
> For skies of couple-colour as a brindled cow;
> For rose-moles all in stipple upon trout that swim;
> Fresh-firecoal chestnut-falls; finches' wings . . .

and concludes,

> Whatever is fickle, freckled (who knows how?)
> He fathers-forth whose beauty is past change;
> . . . .
>   Praise him.[7]

Love of Self

In order to examine what we must do to love ourselves, I will return to something I have said about our relation to God as to a friend. When we are willing to be in the presence of another, faults and all, we accept that person as our friend

---

7. Hopkins, "Pied Beauty," p. 30

and allow him to accept us. Using the same analogy, we see what must be our attitude if we are to love ourselves; we must accept our weaknesses, our faults, our strengths and our accomplishments. It is easy to hate ourselves because we have disappointed ourselves, or our friends, or our God. It takes guts to rebound from such defeats. Does God write us off when we offend him? Does a true friend abandon us when we fail to trust him? Should we curl up and die when we discover that we are weak, or stupid, or unaccepted?

Love is not static; it is not to be squandered, but shared. We cannot begin to share it, however, until we love ourselves enough to conclude that we have something to share.

"Lara's Theme" from the film *Doctor Zhivago* captured the American imagination. When the vocal version of the theme became popular, many a young lover must have felt that the strong and gentle words of the lyrics—"Somewhere my love, there will be songs to sing"—accurately expressed those romantic longings that are so difficult to articulate. But words are meaningless unless they presuppose a place, a voice, a song to sing. Similarly, the sharing of love presupposes a lover of self, a desire to love, and enough love to share. If we were self-sufficient enough not to need reinforcement from God and man, would we be better able to cope with ourselves? I doubt it.

Like the Bensen and Hedges television commercial which depicts a mountain climber whose extra-long cigarette burns the rope which holds him, some of our choices tend to make us crashingly aware that we have made them.

Love Shared

The simple poem "Richard Cory" by Edwin Arlington Robinson has always been particularly poignant to me:

So on we worked, and waited for the light,
And went without the meat, and cursed the bread;
And Richard Cory, one calm summer night,
Went home and put a bullet through his head.[8]

Simon and Garfunkel are the contemporary bards who direct our attention to the tragic Richard Corys of the world, those "most peculiar men" who either live with loneliness and reticence, or die. And who is to blame for such a death? Aren't Richard Cory and so many others who are "not like us," "most peculiar men"?

When Martin Luther King Jr. was shot down in Memphis, who pulled the trigger? Was it not all of us? Do we not create the monsters of society who eventually kill themselves or us? Far from exonerating anyone who might take the life of another human being, I am merely pointing out what I have felt for so very long—the greatest sins are sins of omission. I feel much more sorrow over that which I have failed to do for others, than for anything objectively sinful that I have done. If love is to be shared, then the failure to share,

---

8. Edwin Arlington Robinson, "Richard Cory," in **The American Tradition in Literature** (New York: W. W. Norton and Company, 1967) p. 1042

the failure to give of our time, of our material possession, of ourselves, is the quintessence of failure. One's failure to share always has a history. Had we not, for example, failed as human beings, as Americans, as Christians, to aid the minorities of our nation, much anguish might have been spared so many of our fellow citizens. A man as great-souled as Dr. King might not have had to put his life on the line for the rights of others; a fear-ridden racist might not have had to take it upon himself to shatter the career of one who threatened to make America a country of peaceful cohabitation. Black Panther members might be constructively improving America instead of stockpiling weapons.

The world may never be as it is in the childlike vision of E. E. Cummings "puddle-wonderful"; it may never be wonderful to all men at any time. Yet the world is *de facto* full of wonder for all who will share with others, especially through encouragement to and appreciation of the contributions made by others. The keynote quotation for our discussion of love, "All of us are somehow responsible to everyone for everything," gives us the best clue to the relationship we bear to each other; we are brothers. It was not without purpose that Christ addressed the prayer which He taught us to pray to "Our Father." We are responsible to each other for the progress which we, together, are to make in life. Granted, as a blueprint for action, these lines are pretty fuzzy, but let's start. Is there anyone with whom I come in contact who is alone or in some way alienated from those with whom he works or lives? If I cannot be his friend, can I be, in some small way, his brother?

Love in the World

Mahatma Gandhi once said, "If Christ ever visits India, he had better visit it in the form of bread." He was right. No amount of spiritual counseling, no example of patience can influence a man whose stomach is shouting for food. If we are to consider loving our brothers in the world at large, it might be well to review words written by J. M. Abraham, a Jesuit missionary from Kurseong, India: "Christ's description of the last judgment haunts me. He is not going to quiz me on subtle theological doctrines, he is not going to ask me about my mystical experiences. He is going to put to me (and to you and to all of us) one blunt question: 'I was hungry, did you feed me? I was naked, did you clothe me?'"

Anyone who says he prays for others and never turns a hand to help another who is in need does not have my respect, and probably has little for himself. If Christianity is to mean more than a blanket to cling to, or a shelter for our psyches, then we, the Christians of the world, must make it concrete. Obviously, our country should not be expected to feed and clothe the world, but we certainly should assume the leadership in distributing the affluence of the world on an equitable basis. If this means technological research, technical assistance in other lands, or galvanization of world-wide machinery and utilization of food surpluses, then we should be willing to pay that price. It is not as though we would be pouring resources down a drain. We are, all of us, in this life and on this earth together. The death of a young mother on Cebu or the hunger cry of a child in Laos may not seem to affect me personally, but it does affect my world. And for whose sake am I living anyway? For my sake alone?

There is a tremendous significance in the final scene of *Midnight Cowboy* when the young cowboy has finally let the love of his wet, dirty, underhanded, tubercular friend transform him. Together, these two unlikely friends might forge a new life, a more wholesome life. When Rico dies quite suddenly, Joe is not unnerved, does not mourn for the life that might have been; he sits with his arm around his lifeless friend's shoulder, aware really for the first time that Rico was the only friend he had, if, indeed, he was a friend at all, and reflects on the beauty of the bond that had existed between them. We sometimes do not embrace the exigencies of life until we have embraced the unknown commodity— death.

The questions which I ask as we become codiscoverers of ourselves in an effort to live with the mystery of Christianity are not meant to be condemnatory. They merely articulate thoughts which have puzzled me. Remember, Christ put a few questions to us, and we really haven't answered Him yet (cf. Matthew 25:35-46). He told us, "I have come to cast fire upon the earth, and what would I but that it be ignited?" (Luke 12:49) Maybe if each of us were a Christian fire-lighter, all of us would become inflamed with a desire to pay more than lip service to the countless millions of people who cannot begin to live until we give them something to live for. If we are repelled by their coarseness or their reaction to our apparent patronization, we must look deeper for a beauty that might betray the existence of a humanity very much like our own. Wordsworth notes that:

The meanest flower that blows can give
Thoughts that do often lie too deep for tears.[9]

9. William Wordsworth, "Ode on the Intimations of Immortality," in **Wordsworth's Poems** (New York: Charles Scribner's Sons, 1923) p. 317

CHAPTER II

JOY

"A hum came suddenly into his head, a hum such as is hummed hopefully to others."   Winnie the Pooh

The above quotation captures one of those ineffable realities which we, upon reflection, call "joyful." I particularly like the statement because it includes the idea of hope, and the ideal of sharing with others. Leon Bloy shoots to the heart of the matter when he asserts that "Joy is the most infallible sign of the presence of God." Again, what is more hopeful than that? And where is God more present to us than in other people? The relationship between love and joy is clearly evident in the excerpt from *The Catcher in the Rye* which appeared in the last chapter.

Being joyful does not mean going around turning cartwheels or whistling. There is a radical correlation between Joy and Peace, the topic of my next chapter. For now, though, let's consider a few characteristics of joy. It will be best, I think, to see it in light of its opposite, desolation. You will notice that sadness or sorrow are not contrary to joy; desolation is.

Desolation is that state of separation, real or apparent,

from God who adds the dimension of joy to our lives. If the separation is real, if you or I have turned our backs on God, a degree of guilt may attend our desolation. Strangely, if the separation is only apparent, God may be trying us in order to increase our desire for the true joy and peace that he alone, through persons, can achieve in our souls.

The first definition of joy, then, is awareness of God's presence to us.

Joy radiates purpose. If our lives appear meaningless, we feel anything but joyful. We begin to question our own fulfillment. We feel old.

The joy of youth centers on the wonderful possibilities and potentialities that spread before us. Joy is not the glittering light-show imitation of fulfillment seen in F. Scott Fitzgerald's novel, *The Great Gatsby*. The best example that I have found of the well-integrated man on the brink of fulfillment is Gene Forester in *A Separate Peace*. Only after the crucible of experience teaches him to accept himself as he is, not as some idealization of himself, is he able to confront reality joyfully. The real struggle is to conquer fear of one's potential failure. Within all of us the seeds of greatness and the seeds of destruction can be found. That we have the choice between the two is something for which we should be more than grateful. If we live in fear of that choice, then Hamlet is right, "conscience doth make cowards of us all," but if we dare to be optimists about our inclination and ability to choose well, we will be more like Gene Forester, who could say that "Looking back now across fifteen years, I could see with great clarity the fear I had lived in, which must mean that in the interval I had succeeded in a very important undertaking: I must have made my escape from it."[1]

I think it is important to mention briefly the reason for a young child's joy. The child is indifferent, in the good sense, to life about him. All is new, all is possible. Wonder reigns. The man or woman who is alive to life, and interested in life's possibilities, is fulfilled as a person. He or she is what one calls "a child at heart," a fine description of the mature adult. The people you and I admire most are those who have grown old least perceptibly.

I would here merely hint at the wealth of meaning in Christ's words, "I have come that they may have life, and have it more abundantly" (John 10:10), and "Ask and you shall receive, that your joy may be full" (John 16:24). The full Christian life by implication, is full human life; joy is ours for the asking if we are child enough to receive it.

The irrepressible Walt Whitman may be too effusive for some peoples' tastes, but he cannot be disregarded as an important literary figure, both because his style considerably influenced modern American poetry, and more importantly, because his favorite themes say a great deal to us, or should:

I tramp a perpetual journey (come listen all!)

---

1. John Knowles, **A Separate Peace** (New York: The Macmillan Company, 1959; New York; Bantam Books, 1966) p. 2

My signs are a rainproof coat, good shoes, and a staff
   cut from the woods,
No friend of mine takes his ease in my chair,
I have no chair, no church, no philosophy,
I lead no man to a dinner table, library, exchange,
But each man and woman of you I lead upon a knoll,
My left hand hooking you round the waist,
My right hand pointing to landscapes of continents and
   to the public road.
Not I, not anyone else can travel that road for you,
You must travel it for yourself. . . .
The spotted hawk swoops by and accuses me, he complains
   of my gab and of my loitering.
I too am not a bit tamed, I too am untranslatable,
I sound my barbaric yawp over the roofs of the world. . . .
                              ("Song of Myself")[2]

I'm not sure that those of us who have a chair, a church, a
philosophy, are as willing to express our joy at the wonders
of existence, our joy at the possibilities that lie ahead of us
on "the public road." Perhaps if we were a bit less "tamed"
and "translatable" we would more frequently sound our respective yawps over the roofs of the world. We need both to
hear America singing, and to sing out ourselves. There is
something singularly sad about a country whose majority is

---

2. Walt Whitman, "Song of Myself," in **Leaves of Grass** (New York: New American Library, Signet Edition, 1960) pp. 49 to 96

characterized by silence. Whatever we hold politically or morally can't mean too much to us if we continue to joylessly embalm it.

We hum, it is true, largely to ourselves, but we are not the only ones who listen. Are we so proud as to insist that our unique joy, however it may express itself, is incommunicable; or might it become for others a sign of God's creative presence?

Personal Joy

I hesitate to treat joy under the aspect of "personality," mainly because I have a deep-seated conviction that noncommunicative joy is nonexistent. What I will attempt to do is look at this very real virtue from one person's point of view. What does it mean for me, or for you, to be joyful?

I know that I am full of joy only when I am honestly living my life without affectation or pretense at being something other than what I am. These times are rare. Joy has never been a wholesale proposition. We do not always find ourselves in the state of joyfulness. I merely mean that we know, in retrospect, that our experiences of joy occurred at those moments when we could let ourselves be spontaneous. Spontaneity is an index of growth toward self-hood.

In Rostand's Cyrano de Bergerac, the irrepressible Cyrano asks "what would you have me do?"

Seek for the patronage of some greatness,
And like a creeping vine on a tall tree
Crawl upward, where I cannot stand alone?
No thank you!

A little later he offers his positive response to life:

To sing, to laugh, to dream,
To walk in my own way and be alone,
Free, with an eye to see things as they are,
A voice that means manhood—to cock my hat
Where I choose—at a word, a yes, a no.
To fight—to write. To travel any road
Under the sun, under the stars, nor doubt
If fame or fortune lie beyond the bourne—
Never to make a line I have not heard
In my own heart, yet, with all modesty
To say: "My soul, be satisfied with flowers,
With fruit, with weeds even; but gather them
In the one garden you may call your own."[3]

There are a number of examples of characters "caught" in
their joyfulness in the vibrant musical *Oliver!* but one such
instance is particularly significant when we stop to analyze it.
Oliver stands on the balcony above a street bustling with ac-

---

3. Edmond Rostand, **Cyrano de Bergerac** (New York: Bantam Books,
Brian Hooker translation, 1959) p. 75

tivity and alive with song. Deeply impressed by the beautiful morning, he asks, "Who will tie it up with a ribbon, and put it in a box for me?" It strikes me that genuine joy is precisely that which cannot be bought, tied or boxed. Gifts, which are by their very nature symbolic of the affection of the giver, can be purchased and wrapped; joy cannot. Joy does not symbolize something; it is what it is. It is the reality itself. That is why spontaneous, unstudied response frequently is an index to joy. One does not come away from a joyful experience saying that what he has felt was like something else, or symbolic of something else. It is usually quite enough to have felt damn happy during an experience which might impress no one in the retelling. This might be why C. S. Lewis called his autobiography *Surprized by Joy*.

I am suspicious of any emotion masquerading as joy which one wishes to keep to himself. Self-satisfaction is a nonemotional evaluation of truth, joy is a rejoicing over the truth which cannot be kept to ourselves, because the truth is that we are on this earth, not for ourselves, but for one another. The experiences of joy that you and I have had are God-given, but wasted if they were not shared. Karl Barth's designation of Christ as the "man for others" is of tremendous significance: Christ came into the world in order that we could become more like God by being more truly ourselves, which is another way of saying "growing in Christlikeness." When we accept, as He did, our unique role in life and our relationship with each other, we will be able to suffer what-

ever we must. Remember, it was "with joy set before him"
that He "endured the cross" (Hebrews 12:2).

Joy Shared

G. K. Chesterton says of man that "alone among the animals, he is shaken with the beautiful madness called laughter;
as if he had caught sight of some secret in the very shape of
the universe hidden from the universe itself." If it is true that
humor is but human acknowledgment of incongruity, then
laughter and humor, inasmuch as they share in the manifestation of joy, have the status of "natural virtues." Laughter
and humor are most genuine and unforced when one is in
the presence of a friend—and this is not just coincidence.

Joy shared is friendship. Remember, joy does not exclude
sorrow, occasional sadness, or even a certain salvific anger at
one's own or another's limitations. True friendship and genuine joy involve the acceptance of things as they are, as long
as two or more people are honestly striving to be what each
one *ought* to be in the eyes of God and man. When we are
trying our best, and still haven't "arrived," our reaction should
be joy. The ability to share fears and frustrations and to grow
in the process is an earned privilege of friendship. Alfred
Lord Tennyson probably did not realize the theological significance of his Ulysses' statement:

That which we are, we are—

One equal temper of heroic hearts,
Made weak by time and fate, but strong in will
To strive, to seek, to find, and not to yield.[4]

The striving and refusal to yield in life may be done in isolation, but individualistic action, as Hemingway's "code hero" Santiago learned, only serves to bring home one's need for interdependence and affection. Early in that novel the beautifully simple relationship between Santiago and the boy Manolin is established: "The old man had taught the boy to fish and the boy loved him." A little later the boy exclaims, "There are many good fishermen and some great ones. But there is only you." Finally, after enduring the painful and futile fight to bring the truly great fish back with him, Santiago realizes how much he had missed the boy. Manolin says, "You must get well fast for there is much that I can learn and you can teach me everything. How much did you suffer?" "Plenty," the old man said. His suffering was more of the spiritual than the physical order. By going "too far out" he found out who he was, how old he was, how much he was a needer, how much his joy was dependent upon his sharing himself with his young friend.

By virtue of the Incarnation, there are no purely natural realities. The world, as Pierre Teilhard de Chardin has so well pointed out, has been "Christified." Since Christ has said

4. Alfred Lord Tennyson, "Ulysses" in **Tennyson, Selected Poetry** (New York: Holt, Rinehart and Winston, 1956) p. 85

that wherever two or three have gathered in his name, he is with them, and since friendship is essentially a Christian bond—love, joy, and peace being its sign and substance— genuine friendship, joy shared is an obvious supernaturalization.

In an oration that Dr. Martin Luther King Jr. delivered in 1963 at the Concourse of Colored People in Washington, D.C., he remarked that "I have a dream that one day little black boys and black girls will be able to join hands with little white boys and white girls as sisters and brothers."[5] He didn't say that this would be easy or immediate. He didn't say that the path would skirt sorrow or evade sadness. He didn't say that all doubts and misgivings had been vanquished. But there was joy in his heart at the prospect, there will be joy in the world at its actualization—a joy that will be merely a foreshadowing of that ultimate union of all peoples and all races in Christ.

Joy to the World

It is unfortunate that many of the most significant phrases from Scripture and a number of sacred lyrics have become so hackneyed, secularized, and popularized that they no longer seem to have meaning; it is equally unfortunate that some

---

5. Concourse of Colored People: © 1963 by Martin Luther King, Jr.

of the best contemporary statements in literature and music
have been ignored by those who hold sacred nothing but the
"sacred." The title of this chapter contains a depth and a
beauty which can be appreciated only when one remembers
that Christ's coming, his assuming of our humanity—not out
of condescension as much as out of loving compassion—was
the advent of love, joy, and peace "with us." Emmanuel
means "God present to us." The fact that Christ chose the
natural way to enter the mystery of our world merely im-
presses us with the immensity of the mystery of God's love.

Well, here we are; and the impact of Christ's coming has
diminished considerably over the past two thousand years, or
has it?

A great deal of damage is done by those who would have
Christlikeness enshrined so exclusively in the personages of
"holy" people that the Spirit of the Son of God becomes in-
discernible in the rest of us. Were we to anthropomorphize
God a bit more I don't believe that he would be the least bit
upset to find that some of the most Christian of principles are
currently upheld under non-Christian, not anti-Christian, au-
spices. One of the most articulate of these seeming anomalies
is the American folk song. John Dewey's observation six years
ago, that "If one could control the songs of a nation, one need
not care who made the laws,"[6] is particularly prophetic in

---

6. John Dewey, **Freedom and Culture** (New York: G. P. Putnam's
Sons, p. 10

light of the world of today. I intend to analyze several of the more typical concerns of contemporary lyrical questioners, and then apply their insights to the world scene.

It was Simon and Garfunkel who brought the world's attention to the fact that prophetic words are often written on the subway walls and the halls of tenements — and a number of very sensitive scribblers have given voice to what we have all felt. Many of the social injustices of our time have been satirized in song. The 5th Dimension ushered in the Age of Aquarius, and the Moody Blues keep the song world turning with their searching lyricism.

The Byrds, in "Goin' Back," focus upon one man's growing realization that he must, as an adult member of society, make difficult choices, and yet try to maintain his youthful ideas. He admits that "A little bit of courage is all we lack." He opts to stay young while growing old, his way of "goin' back:"

> Now there are no games
> To only pass the time;
> No more electric trains;
> No more trees to climb—
>> But thinking young and growing older is no sin;
>> And I can't play the game of life to win.[7]

None of us can play the game to life to win. We are not

---

7. GOIN' BACK by Gerry Goffin & Carole King; © 1966, 1967 by Screen Gems-Columbia Music Inc., New York. Used by permission. Reproduction prohibited.

on this earth for ourselves. It took a man like ourselves, to enter into our lives and introduce us to Himself. This was God's gift of Joy to the world, and we can hardly rejoice in that coming if we fail in our human duty to *be* human to each one of our brothers. To do otherwise is to remain a child in the sense of childish; to share our gift is to spread our joy.

One of the most joyful and durable folk ballads over the past decade has been "Scarlet Ribbons" celebrating a charmingly inexplicable gift to a child:

Searched all night, my heart was breaking; just before
   the dawn was breaking,
I peeked in and on her bed, in gay profusion lying there,
Scarlet ribbons, lovely ribbons, scarlet ribbons for her
   hair.
If I live to be a hundred, I will never know from where
Came those ribbons, lovely ribbons, scarlet ribbons for
   her hair.[8]

If today's songs plead for freedom and reform more often than they pray for miracles, it is because youth is impatient to celebrate the miracle of *Now*—and we cannot afford to tune out the music while it is being made.

As strange as it may seem to quote a somewhat stuffy Victorian in support of a transcendental music which has the power to speak to men's souls, Thomas Carlyle gives us a

---

8. **Scarlet Ribbons** by Evelyn Danzig and Jack Segal. Copyright 1949 by Mills Music, Inc.

powerful picture of what happens when prophets and nature itself are rejected.

The Gospel of Dilettantism . . .
Perhaps few narratives in History or Mythology are more significant than that Moslem one, of Moses and the Dwellers by the Dead Sea. A tribe of men dwelt on the shores of that same Asphaltic Lake; and having forgotten as we are all too prone to do, the inner facts of Nature, and taken up with the falsities and outer semblances of it, were fallen into sad conditions—verging indeed towards a certain far deeper Lake. Whereupon it pleased kind Heaven to send them the Prophet Moses, with an instructive word of warning out of which might have sprung 'remedial measures' not a few. But no: the men of the Dead Sea discovered, as the valet-species always does in heroes or prophets, no comeliness in Moses; listened with real tedium to Moses, with light grinning, or with splenetic sniffs and sneers, affecting even to yawn; and signified, in short, that they found him a humbug, and even a bore. Such was the candid theory these men of the Asphalt Lake formed to themselves of Moses, that probably he was a humbug, and certainly he was a bore.

Moses withdrew; but Nature and her rigorous veracities did not withdraw. The men of the Dead Sea, when we next went to visit them, were all 'changed into Apes;' sitting on the trees there, grinning now in the most un-affected manner; gibbering and chattering very genuine nonsense; finding the whole universe now a most indisputable humbug! The Universe has *become* a Humbug to these Apes who thought it one. There they sit and chatter, to this hour: only, I believe, every Sabbath there returns to them a bewildered half-consciousness, half-reminiscence; and they sit, with their wizzened smoke-dried visages, and such an air of supreme tragically as Apes may; looking out through those blinking, smok-bleared eyes of theirs, into the wonderfulest universal smokey twi-light and undecipherable disordered Dusk of Things; wholly an Uncertainty, Unintelligibility, they and it; and for commentary thereon, here and there an unmusical chatter or mew: truest, tragicalest Humbug conceivable by the mind of man or ape! They made no use of their souls; and so have lost them. Their worship on the Sabbath now is to roost there, with unmusical screeches, and half-remember that they had souls.

Didst thou never, O Traveller, fall in with parties of this tribe? Meseems they are grown somewhat numerous in our day.[9]

What Carlyle wrote in 1836 could have been written one hundred and thirty-four years later. It might be that "unmusical screeches" result when songs and lyrics expressive of joy and even critical of society become stifled or stop being listened to.

---

9. Thomas Carlyle, **Past and Present**, Bk. III, Chap. IV (1836)

Currently, ecology and anti-pollutants are "in" terms, off-shore drilling and smog are, hopefully, on the way out. No one, however, believes that nature is going to be restored to its primeval purity overnight. The topicality of discussions over the despoliation of our environment points up an important fact about the value of joy.

"What is honored in a country," wrote Aristotle, "is cultivated there." If Americans truly rejoiced over the natural beauty about them; if they cared more about living life and a little less about making a living, our environment would not be threatening us as it is.

We tend to be very protective once we recognize the threat which technology poses. We forget that technology can be turned to the bettering of human existence, and turned from exploitation. There is, then, an element of risk even in joy. If we care about celebrating the beauty of nature, we must begin to stand up and be counted. If joy in the mystery of human nature is at stake, we must be even more adamant in its defense.

To _____ Date _____

FROM THE DESK OF REV. JOHN M. CARBOY, S.J.

REMARKS:

CHAPTER III

PEACE

"And I, like one lost in a thorny wood,
That rents the thorns and is rent with the thorns,
Seeking the way and straying from the way
Not knowing how to find the open air
But toiling desperately to find it out,
Torment myself. . . ."
Richard, Duke of Glouchester in
Shakespeare's Henry VI, Part III

Restlessness and confusion must be the substitute for *THINK* signs in the antechambers of hell. And yet, a healthy dissatisfaction with one's status quo is a real help toward true peace. Because the words of the Duke of Glouchester in Shakespeare's play are paradoxical, they help us to see both sides of the restlessness-peace conflict. Richard does the worst things for the worst reasons. At one time he is Iago in *Othello,* Heathcliff in *Wuthering Heights,* and Percy Grimm in *Light in August,* He is man choosing his own worst interests.

Richard's struggles lead him to incessant anxiety and, finally, madness. The classic example of the man who confuses self-acceptance and self-hatred, he ultimately rejects everything about himself. He accepts only his torment which he usually relieves by giving a swift sword in the shins to anyone who seems to thwart his quest for the English crown.

We are all restless, which is to say, we are all human. St. Augustine really hit home when he said, "Our hearts were made for Thee, O Lord, and they are restless until they rest in Thee."[1]

There would be neither hawks nor doves were there no wars; there would be no wars were there no Richards and no nations whose ambitions center so much upon themselves because they regard themselves as somehow inferior. Have you ever noticed that the men and women we most respect are the very ones who have become strong and wise in the responsible exercise of the same talents that any number of others possess, but have refused to acknowledge?

When we speak of specifically Christian peace, we must realize that Christ came to bring "not peace but the sword." His presence on earth forced men to take sides, to be responsible for their choices. As a result of his coming, however, every man had greater freedom, and the law of love became the primary norm within the context of man's natural moral apprehensions. Again, as a result of the sword, genuine peace could be a legacy to all who loved the Lord their God and their neighbor for his sake: "Peace is my parting gift to you,

---

1. St. Augustine, **The Confessions of St. Augustine** (New York: Washington Square Press, 1960) p. 1

my own peace, such as the world cannot give. Set your troubled hearts at rest and banish your fears" (John 14:27). An echo of this gift to each of us is heard in St. John's epistle, "There is no fear in love; perfect love banishes fear" (I John 4:18). It is fear that makes both peace and love impossible.

You and I need peace in our lives. We so seldom let ourselves rest in the love of God or the love of others. We so seldom allow ourselves to love ourselves; we so often allow our fears to prohibit us from effectively loving others. Do we actually believe that we can find peace in our madcap world? Or are we afraid to accept anything that might make some future demand on us?

Let's take a concrete example of an opportunity to have peace even while being active: You are driving home on your city's skid row; a man collapses on the sidewalk as you pass by. You are in a hurry to get home to dinner, and not particularly anxious to inconvenience yourself by stopping and trying to assist a man who is probably dead drunk and very likely resentful of any assistance from a patronizing busybody. But . . . you throw caution to the winds, and pull into a parking space, head for the corner, and get the man on his feet. He is very drunk and cannot tell you where he lives or where you might take him to get him out of the 18° weather. The police department sign across the street catches your eye, and the obvious course of action suggests itself to you. Here will be warmth and a meal and a place in which to sober up. You help your unwilling friend across the street and to the sergeant's desk. The police assure you that they will take care of their charge and you depart followed by a string of oaths from the muddled mouth of one you know you helped. But you are at peace.

Had you passed him by, would he or you be any more peaceful than you both were before that very human encounter? Opportunities for bi-lateral peacefulness are the "tide in the affairs of men which—taken at the flood lead on to fortune. . . ."

Sometimes the best way to view the contradictory states or conditions which man is subject to is to think analogically. Many are the writers who have drawn graphic pictures of isolation, that aspect of aloneness which, taken to an extreme, denies the very possibility of genuine peace.

Liam O'Flaherty prints such a scene in "The Wounded Cormorant":

> The other birds, having assured themselves that there was no enemy near, began to look at the wounded one suspiciously. It had its eyes closed, and it was wobbling unstably on its leg. They saw the wounded leg hanging crookedly from its belly and its wings trailing slightly. They began to make curious screaming noises. One bird trotted over to the wounded one and pecked at it. The wounded bird uttered a low scream and fell forward on its chest. It spread out its wings, turned up its beak, and opened it out wide, like a young bird in a nest demanding food.

Immediately the whole flock raised a cackle again and took to their wings. They flew out to sea, high up in the air. The wounded bird struggled up and also took flight after them. But they were far ahead of it, and it could not catch up with them on account of its waning strength. However, they soon wheeled inwards towards the cliff, and it wheeled in after them, all flying low over the water's surface. Then the flock rose slowly, fighting the air fiercely with their long thin wings in order to propel their heavy bodies upwards. They flew half-way up the face of the cliff and alighted on a wide ledge that was dotted with little black pools and white feathers strewn about.

The wounded bird tried to rise too, but it had not gone out to sea far enough in its swoop. Therefore it had not gathered sufficient speed to carry it up to their ledge. It breasted the cliff ten yards below the ledge, and being unable to rise upwards by banking, it had to wheel outwards again, cackling wildly. It flew out very far, descending to the surface of the sea until the tips of its wings touched the water. Then it wheeled inward once more, rising gradually, making a tremendous effort to gather enough speed to take it to the ledge where its comrades rested. At all costs it must reach them or perish. Cast out from the flock, death was certain. Sea-gulls would devour it.

When the other birds saw it coming towards them and

heard the sharp whirring of its wings as it rose strongly, they began to cackle fiercely, and came in close line to the brink of the ledge, darting their beaks forward and shivering. The approaching bird cackled also and came headlong at them. It flopped on to the ledge over their backs and screamed, lying on the rock helplessly with its wings spread out, quite exhausted. But they had no mercy. They fell upon it fiercely, tearing at its body with their beaks, plucking out its black feathers and rooting it about with their feet. It struggled madly to creep in farther on the ledge, trying to get into a dark crevice in the cliff to hide, but they dragged it back again and pushed it towards the brink of the ledge. One bird prodded its right eye with its beak. Another gripped the broken leg firmly in its beak and tore at it.

At last the wounded bird lay on its side and began to tremble, offering no resistance to their attacks. Then they cackled loudly, and, dragging it to the brink of the ledge, they hurled it down. It fell, fluttering feebly through the air, slowly descending, turning round and round, closing and opening its wings, until it reached the sea.

Then it fluttered its wings twice and lay still. An advancing wave dashed it against the side of the black rock and then it disappeared, sucked down among the seaweed strands.[2]

---

2. Liam O'Flaherty, "The Wounded Cormorant" in **Stories of Liam O'Flaherty** (New York: The Devin Adair Company, 1956)

Do we not reward those who have caused us by their plight to fear our own security much in the manner of the healthy birds who persecute their dying brother?

Peace With Self

Few people are deeply at peace with themselves, and I think that the cause is a kind of mass neurosis carefully cultivated by technologically advanced societies. Every new thrust in the direction of discovery seems to sadly retard each individual's discovery of how to live with himself.

In 1947 Ellison wrote a novel, *Invisible Man,* which very powerfully stated the ambivalent position of the Blacks in America. The novel won the National Book Award for fiction in 1965. Far from a self-pitying complaint, this book captures the correlation between personal disorientation and societal blindness. The following passage points out the sort of sickness which we all experience, and which we all must overcome in order to reinstate that peace we enjoyed as children— at that point in our personal history when we knew security, and were confident even when it seemed threatened:

> You go along for years knowing something is wrong, then suddenly you discover that you're as transparent as air. At first you tell yourself that it's all a dirty joke, or that it's due to the "political situation." But deep down you come to suspect that you're yourself to blame, and you stand naked and shivering before the millions of eyes who look

through you unseeingly. That is the real soul-sickness, the spear in the side, the drag by the neck through the mob-angry town, the Grand Inquisition, the embrace of the maiden, the rip in the belly with the guts spilling out, the trip to the chamber with the deadly gas that ends in the oven so hygienĩcally clean—only it's worse because you continue stupidly to live. But live you must, and you can either make passive love to your sickness or burn it out and go on to the next conflicting phase.[3]

No amount of salve can soothe some wounds. If it is true that most neuroses can be cured by restoring a sense of self value and confidence in one plagued by fears, it is also true that the therapy that most of us need in our day to day disturbances and conflicts is a broader based self-concept—not a false notion of self, but a realistic picture of self in broad perspective. We usually prefer to dwell upon our inadequacies. Let's begin to minimize the debits and maximize the things that we do have going for us. Not everyone has the leisure to paddle a canoe through the calm and calming waters of a lake. Few are the glider pilots who can extricate themselves from the human traffic jam. But many of us can, as Ellison suggests, burn out the sickness and "go on to the next conflicting stage." In each succeeding conflict we will be better able to seek peaceful resolution if we have already ac-

---

3. Ralph Ellison, **Invisible Man** (New American Library, Signet Edition, c 1952 by Ralph Ellison) p. 498

cepted the fact that it was personal strength and purpose which propelled us through the phases which are now part of our wake.

In the justly famous "Symphony" chapter of *Moby Dick,* that single-minded chaser of the "ungraspable phantom of life," Ahab, comes very close to giving up his diabolical quest for Moby Dick when, in conversation with Starbuck, he looks into the firstmate's human eye. Ahab admits that "a forty years' fool has old Ahab been"—forty years spent on the sea, away from the "mild blue days . . . home in Nantucket." As Ahab looks into "the magic glass" of Starbuck's eye, he sees his young wife, and his son, but, Ahab's glance is averted once again. He asks with great anguish:

> What is it, what nameless, inscrutable, unearthly thing is it; what cozening, hidden lord and master, and cruel, remorseless emperor commands me; that against all natural lovings and longings, I so keep pushing, and crowding, and jamming myself on all the time; recklessly making me ready to do what in my own natural heart I durst not so much as dare? Is Ahab, Ahab?[4]

Later, on the second day of the chase, he will admit, "Ahab is forever Ahab, man!" Paradoxically, it is Ahab's overweaning pride which makes him Ahab, and which destroys the "nat-

4. Herman Melville, **Moby Dick** (New York: W. W. Norton Company, 1967) p. 444-445

ural heart" of the powerful figure. It is as difficult for us to "nail down" or "label" Ahab as it is for Ahab to harpoon Moby Dick, the one act which he feels will bring him peace. Even Ahab, Melville tells us, "has his humanities."

This much we can do: we can learn from Ahab the folly of trying to absolutize the confusion and suffering in our lives, and then dispose of it in a single mighty thrust. We can learn to find peace at the core of the turbulency around us; we can learn to accept a certain amount of ambiguity in our lives, never allowing it to so obsess us that natural, human considerations become lost in the shuffle. Many are the Ahabs, and many are the white whales which catch the eye and lead us so far from ourselves that to pursue them is to become someone else, or an aspect of ourselves which when in control is constructive, but run rampant is destructive of our own peace and that of others.

Peace With Others

In today's world the greatest stumbling block to peace is intolerance, and yet intolerance, at least to some degree, is necessary if change is to be effected. This dilemma is brought into bold relief by Flannery O'Connor in her appropriately entitled short-story, "All that Rises Must Converge." The story involves a young man's righteous indignation over his mother's patronizing attitude toward blacks whom she insists she is unprejudiced toward. The son is almost exultant when she is taught a lesson by a huge Negress whose little boy is offered a shiny new penny by the white woman so wed to her prejudice that she cannot realize an idea so sophisticated as tokenism. Her son critically assesses the darkness he perceives his mother dwelling in:

> The old lady was clever enough and he thought that if she had started from any of the right premises, more might have been expected of her. She lived according to the laws of her own fantasy world, outside of which she had never set foot. The law of it was to sacrifice herself for him after she had first created the necessity to do so by making a mess of things. If he had permitted her sacrifices, it was only because her lack of foresight had made them necessary.[5]

He sits with her on the bus, hoping to "teach her a lesson" about reality, particularly the reality that he feels she must face before all others, that the frusrated rage of black people was direced at whites like his mother who pretend that white racism will always be tolerated because it is basically quite moral. When the black woman enters the bus with her little boy, and is discovered to be wearing a hat identical to his mother's, Julian rejoices at the poetic justice of it all. When

---

5. Flannery O'Connor, "Everything That Rises Must Converge," from **Everything That Rises Must Converge** (New York: Farrar, Straus & Giroux, Inc.; reference here is to **Strategies in Prose,** New York: Holt, Rinehart and Winston, Inc., 1968) p. 157

the Negress hits his mother, exclaiming that her little boy "don't take nobody's pennies," Julian decides to ram the lesson home to his bewildered mother:

> "Don't think that was just an uppity Negro woman," he said. "That was the whole colored race which will no longer take your condescending pennies. That was your black double. She can wear the same hat as you, and to be sure," he added gratuitously (because he thought it was funny), "it looked better on her than it did on you. What all this means," he said, "is that the old world is gone. The old manners are obsolete and your graciousness is not worth a damn." "You aren't who you think you are," he said.[6]

It was only when Julian's mother refused to let him take her home, and, crumpling, fell to the pavement, her face fiercely distorted, that he realized that he had by his intolerance, his desire to subject her to a lesson, destroyed something so fundamental to human life that she could not face life without it: her human dignity. The irony of the new reality before him seemed to sweep him back to her, "postponing from moment to moment his entry into the world of guilt and sorrow." Peace can sometimes only be achieved in the crucible of experience, and only when our prejudices and intolerance are

---

6. O'Connor, p. 164

held up to the light, and seen for what they are, evaluated for what they can do.

In order to be at peace with others the trust-level must be high. Invariably, we experience — perhaps when we least expect it—that we have been "sold out." Of course our trust-level drops; our peace has been shattered.

Jean-Paul Marat, a prototype for all revolutionaries, states the age-old frustration in a classic example:

Our minister of war
whose integrity you never doubted
has sold the corn meant for our armies
for his own profit to foreign powers
and now it feeds the troops
who are invading us.[7]

Granted, we can be sold out; our minister of war's integrity may tarnish. The question of peaceful relationships with others, however, depends so much upon our way of looking at things that I believe suspicious natures can almost always find something to justify the suspicion, and less critical appraisers of other persons generally find their optimism rewarded. The most reasonable way to respond to breaches of confidence or lapses in integrity is with anger or indignation,

---

7. Peter Weiss, **The Persecution and Assassination of Jean-Paul Marat as Performed by the Inmates of the Asylum of Charenton Under the Direction of the Marquis de Sade** (New York: Atheneum, 1967) p. 74

and with understanding. If the incident were allowed to cloud one's balanced vision of ordinary human behavior, the result could be far more tragic than the initial circumstance warranted. Life is too big, too wonderful to constrict into the tiny outlook of distrust.

Joanne Woodward sensitively portrayed in *Rachel, Rachel* a thirty-eight year old school teacher caught up in the conventionality of a small town. Her life was ruled by a simpering, possessive mother who thought more of her own needs than of Rachel's. Rachel, plagued by loneliness, and desperate for any release from her psychological bondage, confronted reality, was hurt, came away shaken. The important thing was that she had the courage to act upon the knowledge her hard experiences gave her about herself. I think that the most important aspect of Rachel's final statement upon leaving for another city is not just her realistic acceptance of her own probable future, but her realization that she is not very different from all persons at any time: "My children will probably always be temporary, to be held only for a time, but . . . aren't everybody's?"

Our trust, and consequently, our peace with others, grows as our recognition of and appreciation of similarities in human situations increases.

World Peace

A June 10, 1969 presentation of "60 Minutes" hi-lighted the sad struggle between Nigeria and Biafra, a conflict that could have ended in genocide for the game but starving Ibo tribesmen of Biafra. On the same program students from an all-Black Brooklyn gradeschool were shown singing their way through the touching Jewish musical drama, *Fiddler On the Roof*. Whatever might have been the conflict of ideologies in the recent New York City school strike, for the moment, the tensions were eased in song. The impact of such resolution was all the more dramatic in light of the earlier commentary on the Nigerian-Biafran civil war.

The complexity of a Middle East crisis or a Vietnam war, the potentiality in a Red Chinese-Soviet border skirmish or Tokyo riot defy any neat solutions or pat formulas. A clue, though, to the easing of friction might be found in a very symbolic incident recorded in St. Luke's Gospel. Christ and his disciples had just crossed the lake, and landed at a site just opposite Galilee. After exorcizing the devils from a man who had been a raving maniac, Luke tells us that Jesus "could hardly breathe for the crowds." Among the people hoping to be cured of their infirmities was a woman who "had suffered from hemorrhages for twelve years; and nobody had been able to cure her. She came up from behind and touched the edge of his cloak, and at once her hemorrhage stopped" (Lk. 8:42-48). Jesus knew immediately that someone had touched him—and I believe that he knew he had been touched in a much more profound way than by mere physical contact. "The woman, seeing she was detected, came trembling and fell at his feet. Before all the people she explained why she had touched him and how she had been instantly cured. He said to her, "My daughter, your faith has cured you. Go in peace.'" Her faith had cured her; but was not he, for all that she knew, a gifted man doing God's work. She could hardly have believed that this man was one with the Father, fully God and fully man. Her faith was, I maintain, in man — and in the power of God to work through men.

Whatever has been said about the necessity for trust, an outlook of realistic optimism, and faith in God's power manifesting itself through human beings, must be part of every country's national perspective if true peace is to ever be more than sheer hypothesis and a wistful dream. The world cries out for men of integrity and vision, Christian vision. Christ was the first, best revolutionary. If E. E. Cummings can salute the raucous bluejay as "you beautiful anarchist," how much more deserving of the title are the men of vision, the peacemakers of the world, the hems of whose garments (speaking symbolically) need but be touched with a gesture affirming faith in man, for hemorrhage to cease?

CHAPTER IV

PATIENCE

*He disliked bars and bodegas. A clean, well-lighted cafe was
a very different thing. Now, without thinking further, he
would go home to his room. He would lie in bed and finally,
with daylight he would go to sleep. After all, he said to
himself, it is probably only insomnia. Many must have it.*[1]

A waiter in Hemingway's

A CLEAN, WELL-LIGHTED PLACE.

Patience is a virtue, but when it makes of one a patsy, it
becomes counter-productive. The highly satirical movie *Bob
and Carol and Ted and Alice* presents the viewer with patience reduced to the absurd. First the husband, then his wife,
have love affairs, confess their aberrations, meet with patience
and understanding which stems from an in-depth experience
with sensitivity training, and continue to love one another
without rancor. The implication in the satire is that gut-level,
or feeling-level relationships which lead persons to pretend
that honesty is a greater virtue than mutual love and respect,

---

1. Ernest Hemingway, **The Short Stories of Ernest Hemingway**
(New York: Charles Scribner's Sons, 1953) p. 383

are pure fantasy. We should never lie down and play dead in the name of patience.

"Patience" may come from the Latin verb for suffering, but it need not imply enduring. Patience is an endearing quality, our acceptance of what is *because* it is. And yet patience is also positive. It is "constructive" or "creative" patience in another which really grabs me. Again, it is as teacher that each of us especially exercise this sort of creativity. Gabriel Moran wisely observes that "the worst thing about a teacher despairing of a student is that it may lead the student to despair of himself.[2]

The statement from Hemingway's beautifully written story quoted above, is made by a remarkably compassionate man. His awareness belies his words; he is quite cognizant of the isolation of his situation. He accepts what he suspects many others must endure. And not only that, he helps others, earlier in the story, to endure greater loneliness than his own. I am reminded of Thomas Mann's observation in *Death in Venice:* "To be poised against fatality, to meet adverse conditions gracefully is more than simple endurance; it is an act of aggression, a positive triumph."

We all must accept with a degree of equanimity a great many of life's subtle but certain blows. If our patience extends no further, though, it is neither Christian nor virtue.

There is no virtue in accepting what we should change,

2. Gabriel Moran, **Vision and Tactics Toward and Adult Church** (New York: Herder and Herder, 1968) p. 107

and less in keeping external composure while we writhe internally.

Christian patience, it seems to me, involves doing the best with what we have for whomever we meet, and when we are thwarted, accepting our own inadequacies while remaining open to possibilities. Christ's patience is the perfect example of what ours must be. It was big enough to embrace betrayal and crucifixion, and human enough to rebel at desecration. It is genuine enough to allow for the countless false starts of a world of "other Christs" who cannot accept themselves as weak but necessary extensions of Himself.

A beautiful example of realistic patience is portrayed in *A Man and a Woman,* Claude Lalouche's brilliant film. The man has lost his wife in a sad, precipitous suicide, and the woman has lost her husband in a freak accident. Both had been deeply and ingenuously in love. Sometime after the tragedies the two meet at the school where his son and her daughter are boarded. A restrained infatuation occurs as each allows the other to intrude upon his and her loneliness. Near the end of the film both the man and the woman admit that their former happiness keeps them from fully enjoying a potentially complementary arrangement with life. A period of isolation results before the two embrace each other again, and together they are able to embrace a whole new world of possibilities. Even in this final frame of the film, though, a look of painful sadness is caught in the woman's face, a symbol, I believe, of an acceptance of two loves, that of the first man and that of the second. Such acceptance of unresolved tension is the key to living and the very sign of patience.

Patience and acceptance have thus far been discussed in their natural aspects, and grace does build on nature. Let's consider how "interiorized" or "supernaturalized" patience manifests itself.

Do you remember Christ's instruction to forgive one who has wronged you as often as "seventy times seven" times? Well, he not only preached this sort of patience, he practiced it. Many are the Mary Magdalens and Apostles Paul who have been accepted with their faults and made saints. Do we, by our patience, accept what we seemingly cannot change, and constructively criticize what ought to be reevaluated or reinvigorated?

And when it comes to ourselves, can we accept—patiently —what we cannot avoid, while striving to be our own "best selves?" Let's be realistic; we are weak and very, very human, but we are not the absolute clods we sometimes, quite un-Christianly, delight in crying to ourselves about.

Patience with Self

I am convinced that it is rather futile to ask "Why am I me?" or "Why am I even here to worry about it?" Hopkins says, "What I *do* is me; for that I came."[3] Patience requires not just an acceptance of myself, of whomever I happen to be, but also of what I do. Archibald MacLeish's play, *J.B.*,

---

3. Hopkins, "As Kingfishers . . ." as in Introduction, p. 53

speaks that fact rather forcefully. J.B.'s words should remind us of the Dostoevsky statement quoted in the chapter on Love. J. B.'s realization of his responsibility is unequivocal.

> I'd rather suffer
> Every unspeakable suffering God sends,
> Knowing it was I that suffered,
> I that earned the need to suffer,
> I that acted, I that chose,
> Than wash my hands with yours in that
> Defiling innocence. Can we be men
> And make an irresponsible ignorance
> Responsible for everything? I will not
> Listen to you![4]

The fact is that we are ourselves, we are living, breathing components of a world that screams for individuality in the face of multiplicity. What would happen if we accepted ourselves, and tried to go from there? Acceptance—there's the problem. Americans find it hard to accept themselves as a nation because assassinators have snuffed out the lives of men who have loved their country enough to criticize it. Will you and I ever come to grips with the assassinator within ourselves who so often lashes out at elements in our lives which threaten our security, bare our inadequacies, convict us of cowardice, or mock our pretentiousness?

4. Archibald MacLeish, **J.B.** (Cambridge, Mass: Houghton Mifflin Company, 1956) p. 123

You might conclude from the critical tone of my questioning that I espouse impatience with one's self, not patience. Well, are they really so different? We live with contradiction. Let's hope that we never lose the ability to surprise ourselves. If we do, we will have stopped growing, stopped living. T. S. Eliot is not brooding when he discovers that "Every moment is a new and shocking valuation of all we have been."[5]

Saul Bellow's lovable sufferer, Herzog, has a difficult time accepting some of the trials of his life. He does, however—and this is the key to his success as a human—accept himself. Bellow tells us how his hero has learned to live with himself:

> The conversation was over, and Herzog returned to the storm windows in the shadow and green damp of the back yard—to his obscure system of idiosyncrasies. A person of irregular tendencies, he practiced the art of circling among random facts to swoop down on the essentials. He often expected to take the essentials by surprise, by an amusing stratagem. But nothing of the sort happened as he maneuvered the rattling glass, standing among the frost-scorched drooping tomato vines tied to their stakes with strips of rag. The plant scent was strong. He continued to feel crippled. He dreaded the depths of feeling he would eventually have to face, when he could no longer call upon his eccentricities for relief.[6]

5. Eliot, **The Four Quartets,** "East Coker," p. 13
6. Saul Bellow, **Herzog** (Greenwich, Conn: Fawcett Publications, Inc., 1965) p. 16

How many of us are that honest? How many of us admit and accept our sheltering eccentricities?

Yes, acceptance is the problem. The more you expect from yourself, the more difficult it is to accept your inability to live up to your expectations. Because, as John Stuart Mill points out, "the refuge of the scoundrel is generality," I had better get down to cases.

I am studying for the priesthood, writing a book on creative Christianity, and teaching English, and, hopefully, Applied Christianity to high school boys. I find often, really more frequently than I stop to reflect on it, that many of the people with whom I come in contact are more priestly, more creatively Christian, and better able to instruct youth than I am. This realization would be terribly discouraging were I not aware of the fact that most priests and educators feel some inadequacy, have some misgivings. In my more rational moments I try to keep thanking God for what he is able to accomplish through me. I guess that it would be presumption to refuse to be an instrument, though perhaps a chipped or defective one, when he is willing to use what he chooses. St. Paul asks, "Does the object moulded say to the one who moulded it: Why hast thou made me thus?" (Romans 9:20)

You and I must present the gift of ourselves to an understandably indifferent world, patient in the realization that there's a little good in the worst of us, and a little bad in the best of us, and a history of fits and starts, rights and wrongs, which have made us what we are. I prefer to think of our lives as realizable potentialities, not unfortunate wastes.

Again, Hopkins, whose whole life required great patience and greater faith in order to counter opposition to what must have been a disarmingly individualistic personality, writes:

> Natural heart's ivy, patience masks
> Our ruins of wrecked past purpose. . . .
> We hear our hearts grate on themselves: it kills
> To bruise them dearer. Yet the rebellious wills
> Of us we do bid God bend to Him even so.[7]

Patience with Others

There is a sense in which Joyce's Stephen Dedalus in *Ulysses* is right; God is a "shout in the street." And there is a sense in which Sartre's hero in *No Exit* is correct; "hell is other people." In the first instance one might focus on the dynamic reality of God with us, among us, in each of us, and thus be saved from rashly dismissing this brilliant writer as "wrong," or "sacrilegious," or "blasphemous." In the second case, one might note that a sensitive person's relationships with others can be the source of great joy, while non-relationship, pettiness, pride, intolerance, and prejudice can create a hell on earth which must approximate that state of eternal isolation from God which we believe hell to be. Such a reflec-

---

7. Hopkins, "Patience, hard thing! the hard thing but to pray," p. 66

tion might lead one to suspect that both James Joyce and Jean-Paul Sartre — and perhaps many other men whose opinions infuriate or profoundly shake us — should be read with openness, not written off out of hand.

Patience is required in one who would discern elements of truth in statements which are difficult to digest; a degree of tolerance must characterize truly Christian responses to life in its diversified manifestations.

When John F. Kennedy, Martin Luther King Jr., and Robert Kennedy were stricken down in the prime of their lives, the world mourned. All three were victims of an intolerance that had turned to hate. And hate, whether or not it results in physical violence, bespeaks death.

The authorized edition of the *Dutch Catechism* defines patience as "very close to hope. It means to be on the watch, lovingly but soberly, to note every spark of goodness in the acts of others and every spark of truth in their words. It is without bitterness and without rancor." The authors conclude that "in the groping efforts of mankind God's visage is gradually revealed more clearly, as we move toward the great revelation of Jesus, who is the human visage of God for us."[8] In the virtue of nonviolence, it seems to me, lies the hope for our world. Christ was himself the most patient of men. Each one of us can personally attest to the patience that God has had with each of us, the most prodigal of sons.

---

8. **A New Catechism: Catholic Faith for Adults** (New York: Herder and Herder, 1967) pp. 299-300

One virtue which necessarily aids our patience is our respect. If we are willing to let another person be, and perhaps even appreciate the fact that he is going his way, which might not be our way, then we will not get particularly hung up over his unique approach to an issue. As Thoreau says:

If a man does not keep pace with his companions,
perhaps it is because he hears a different drummer.
Let him step to the music which he hears, however
measured or far away.

In William Golding's *Lord of the Flies,* which is more a sociological study than a novel in the strict sense, two symbols of peace and order, Ralph's conch shell and Piggy's spectacles, are recognized as emblems of status. Once the glasses have been shattered, nothing is left but anarchy. When Piggy's life is taken, "Ralph wept for the end of innocence, the darkness of man's heart, and the fall through the air of the true, wise friend called Piggy."[9]

Innocence is still in evidence, the hearts of men are not yet darkened, and wise, true friends still exist for each of us. Will we always be able to say this? Is our posture of patience such that we discern the sparks of goodness and truth in all men, even our enemies?

Perhaps the most difficult aspect of Christianity for to-

---

9. William Golding, **The Lord of the Flies** (New York: Capicorn Books, G. P. Putnam's Sons, 1959) p. 186

day's rugged individualist to accept is the principle of "turning the other check" to one's enemy. There is a time and a place for violence, as Christ himself demonstrated to the moneychangers in the temple, but genuine tolerance, creative patience, demands courage. If I take bodily punishment rather than back down on a Christian principle, I am anything but a coward. Patience with others need not always be a sort of martyrdom, but I think it is helpful to respect the high tolerance level of those whom we honor by the name martyr. Without them, the world could not continue toward the day when tolerance will give way to mutual love. Man will not only "endure," Faulkner maintains in his Nobel Prize Acceptance speech, "he will prevail."

The World, Our Patient

Tensions—physical, emotional, psychic, cosmic—find their resolution in family. Before this statement is condemned as simplistic, let's look at the facts. The section of the *Dutch Catechism* entitled "Education for Manhood and Womanhood" contains a beautiful tribute to the power of parental example and union in relieving certain of their children's major anxieties. "Where relationships between the parents are warm, and where the children have the joy of witnessing spontaneous expressions of affection, the most important element of sexual education is assured. The children grow up in an atmosphere where love between man and woman is taken for granted."

The authors go on to say that "Their whole life, giving and receiving, must demonstrate love to the child. Later information about their most intimate intercourse, which is also a form of giving and receiving, will not be shocking revelations."[10] I have quoted this source at length because I firmly believe that family love and mutual respect for unique ways of growing is the best human paradigm for strong, warm, uninhibited, yet restrained living.

I was recently struck by statements made in three movies, one French, one Swedish, one British, concerning irresponsibility toward one's family. The varied treatments of this failure are symptomatic of an attitude of more cosmic proportions.

In *Le Bonheur* (Happiness), a vibrant, affectionate young Frenchman is seen with his wife and children in a beautifully orchestrated vignette. The mood of happiness is so ecstatically portrayed that it seems unreal. The sincerity of the relationship, however, is important to note. In the course of time the young husband, while on a carpentry job in another city, meets a woman very much like his wife. With characteristic exuberance he arranges to make this lovely young widow his mistress. He feels no compunction for his wife and family because, as he later unashamedly states to his wife, he has "so much love to give." At the conclusion of the film his wife, clearly unable to accept her husband's urge for what he believes to be complete self-fulfillment, drowns herself. The husband does the natural thing in these unnatural

---

10. **A New Catechism**, p. 406

circumstances, and without reservation asks his mistress to become the mother of his children.

In the film *Elvira Madigan* a young Swedish army officer deserts his family and his profession and elopes with a beautiful tight-rope ballerina. With childlike abandon the two frolic through most of the film, catching butterflies and making love, until the very real exigency of hunger forces reality upon them. A fellow soldier seeks out the officer and reminds him of obligations at home, but he admits that when one lies in the meadow, the blade of grass nearest the eye is all that is seen. The film ends with two gunshots, the first into the skull of the wistful Elvira, the other, though the viewer does not witness it, into the officer's brain by his own hand.

In both of the above instances, responsible, and therefore genuine, relationships of love were not in evidence; in both cases the results were tragic, and particularly tragic because they are typical. Where the giving and receiving for which each man was created is ignored, and emotionality replaces rationality, chaos prevails.

The full flowering of irresponsibility is evident in *Charley Bubbles,* the film-tableau depicting a young writer's simultaneous material success and his disintegration as a personality. When he visits his wife and his little boy, their needs and his own personal needs conflict, and he finds himself wishing that he had more say in how his son is being brought up. Unfortunately, he has chosen to relinquish that right. The final scene shows Charley releasing one the sandbags of an aerial balloon which he opts to ascend in, whether to obtain a higher viewpoint or to symbolically escape reality, we are not told. The tragedy or irresponsibility, though, is almost tangible.

The responsibility that we have to our world is accented when we consider that it is patient, waiting for us to help realize its potentialities. It is obvious that patience and tolerance, as we have already considered them, are but steps toward resolving the tensions that often distract us from the business of establishing bonds. Lawrence Ferlinghetti draws a graphic picture of what it means to live outside an atmosphere of love. Whether he had in mind the love of union and understanding which I see as the hope and necessity of our yearning world is unimportant. This poem is a parable as poignant as any found in Scripture:

> Cast up
>> the heart flops over
>>> gasping 'Love'
> a foolish fish which tries to draw
>> its breath from flesh of air
> And no one there to hear its death
>> among the sad bushes
> where the world rushes by
>> in a blather of asphalt and delay.[11]

11. Lawrence Ferlinghetti, "25," in **A Coney Island of the Mind,** Copyright 1958 by Lawrence Ferlinghetti, by permission of New Directions Publishing Corporation.

CHAPTER V

KINDNESS

*"Linus (to Snoopy). In regard to animals week, I
have a question...you animals expect to be treated a little
bit nicer by people this week...right? Well, does this mean
that you, in turn are also going to make an extra effort to be
more kind to that cat who lives next door?"*

*Snoopy (lying deep in thought and flat on his back upon his
doghouse roof.) "I hate questions like that."*

Peanuts, CREATED BY CHARLES
SCHULZ; UNITED FEATURE
SYNDICATE, MAY 8, 1969

Linus may have been a bit of an idealist when he made
his query of Snoopy, but his disconcerting logic should make
realists of us all.

Holden Caulfield idealistically tried to erase all of the
four-letter words from the washroom walls of the world. He
made up in compassion what he lacked in realism. Both
Snoopy and Holden are at least opting for what they take to
be kindness, but it might be well to focus on the more
practical aspects of genuine kindness.

The kind man does not dispense band-aids, he cleans wounds. A Spanish Jesuit, recently appeared on a television broadcast from his mission in India. The camera focused on the priest who was giving a sermon to a crowd of squatting, white-clad Indian farmers. His words were simultaneously translated for us, as we sat in comfortable chairs wishing that our aluminum beer cans would not sweat so much. His words were simple, and they were Christian — though he never mentioned Christ. His message went something like this: "Some months back I came to you, and told you that I had two hundred rupees with which to drill a well for irrigation of your crops. Ten men asked for wells; two hundred rupees could pay for just one. So I gave the money to the first man, whose crops were so fine the next year that he was able to pay back the rupees to me, so that I might give them to the second farmer, and so on until ten wells had been drilled, and still I had my original sum of two hundred rupees. That, gentlemen, is a miracle." He went on to say that by their generosity in repaying the money loaned, many families had been able to eat adequately, and still more families, by the same miracle of generosity, would be helped.[1]

It strikes me that some very practical Christian principles might be discerned in the work of this one priest laboring at a task which, at first glance, might seem unpriestly. This man

---

1. Rev. Vincent Ferrer, S.J. "In the Name of God," produced by Joseph Secondari

was truly, Christianly kind insofar as he alleviated the natural needs of his parishioners by making it possible for them to eat. He also taught them Christianity by insisting that they repay him in order that others might share the good fortune. Finally, those who received his charity were not made to feel patronized; the drilling of the wells became a community project, and the continuance of the project became a matter of pride to everyone involved. The "building up of the body of Christ" was, in that priest's mission, a matter of sweat, and it is a lesson to us all.

Literature is full of stories of isolated, unhappy people whom a little kindness might have freed from the dungeons they dug for themselves. Katherine Mansfield deftly sketches two such people in "Dill Pickle," the title referring to a moment of sharing which was appreciated as such by the man involved, but never capitalized upon. In "The Rockinghorse Winner" D. H. Lawrence depicts the tragedy which attends a family's preoccupation with money, and its failure to supply the affection and kindness which a young boy craved. Ivan Bunin's "A Gentleman from San Francisco" is another such example of self-centered climbing, the obverse of kindness.

Speaking positively, Atticus Finch, the hero of Harper Lee's novel, *To Kill a Mockingbird*, takes concrete measures to insure that justice be done to a Negro in a hate-filled southern city. Again, the remarkable Fellini film, *La Strada*, is a sensitive study in kindness proferred by a simple girl, Gelsomina, to her scoundrel master, Zampano. Always, it is

the constructive nature of kindness which causes us to re-
examine our own sometimes sterile disposition to help, and
failure to aid effectively.

William Butler Yeats' poem, "A Prayer for My Daughter," expresses well the priority of kindness over beauty: He
prays that she will not:

> ... consider beauty a sufficient end,
> Lose natural kindness and maybe
> The heart-revealing intimacy
> That chooses right, and never find a friend.[2]

The best way, however, to see the many facets of Christian kindness, is to look at Christ's kindly constructiveness.
Many are the examples of eyes opened, bodies healed, and
tongues made to speak, but the greatest miracles were performed among his own disciples whom he was kind enough
to reprimand, to trust, and to befriend.

A hard lesson to learn is that when we do everything we
can for a person, we usually diminish his dignity and draw
his inadequacies to his attention. Christ had that unique
ability to draw the weak to heights they never felt capable
of, and it is part of the ongoing mystery of Incarnation that
he continues to work in us, always allowing us to accept or
reject his presence. There is a lifetime of meditation in the

2. William Butler Yearts, "A Prayer for my Daughter" from **Selected
Poems and Two Plays of William Butler Yeats**, ed. M. L. Rosenthal,
(New York: Collier Books (MacMillan), 1962) p. 192

words which Paul wrote to the Corinthians: "My brothers, think what sort of people you are, whom God has called. Few of you are men of wisdom, by any human standard; few are powerful or highly born. Yet, to shame the wise, God has chosen what the world counts as folly, and to shame what is strong, God has chosen what the world counts weakness. He has chosen things low and contemptible, mere nothings, to overthrow the existing order. And so there is no place for human pride in the presence of God. You are in Christ Jesus by God's act, for God has made him our wisdom; in him we are consecrated and set free" (1 Corinthians 1:26-30).

God's kindness is such that he might make the Snoopys and the Holden Caulfields of the world constructive idealists, and all of us stumbling disciples of a kind Lord.

Personal Kindness

We fudge. We shorten our steps to avoid the cracks in the sidewalk. We modify our opinions out of human respect. We create crises sometimes because hang ups are popular. Nowhere do we fudge more than in the area of personal kindness — and it must be personal to be kindness at all. By fudging in this area I mean we compromise ourselves time after time to keep from being thought of as a soft touch. I have said before that the greatest sins are sins of omission.

What does it mean to be personally kind? It means to bring your unique personal touch to a person who is suffering, no matter how trivially. John Leary, S.J., past President of Gonzaga University in Spokane, Washington, describes passion as something "undergone." We are all susceptible to insecurity, sadness, frustration; when someone, through interest or constructive companionship shares these passions with us, we are reassured, resurrected.

Helen Keller has passed from this earth, and with her have gone the charm, optimism, and sense of purpose which she both possessed and inspired. But where would the Helen Kellers of the world be without the Annie Sullivans to act as ears and mouths sensitive to the beauty of life about us?

Paul Simon wrote the lyrics to "Dangling Conversation" with sensitivity and candor. Realizing that it takes two to make a conversation, he knew that kissing shadows, not knowing who one's friend is or where he or she is "at," makes for non-relationship, not friendship. It is in this context that dangling conversations or superficial sighs become borders of human lives.

The theme of friendship has been treated with perception by other contemporaries. Whether one defines friendship as C. S. Lewis does in *The Four Loves;* or portrays its depth and ironies as John Knowles does in *A Separate Peace;* or recommends it, as the Beatles do in "I'll Get Along with a Little Help from my Friends" or studies its dissolution as Simon and Garfunkel do in "Old Friends," one fact emerges: There must be a giving and a receiving in a genuine friendship. Fundamentally, personal kindness is the actuation of a predisposition to give to another, to fill up another's need, whether he be young or old, rich or poor, white or black,

Christian, Jew or Muslim. Paul Simon draws attention to this in "Old Friends:" "How terribly odd to be seventy." How terribly odd to find ourselves in any condition foreign to us or uncomfortable for us. How terribly sad to be left in that condition. Charley Brown, Charles Schulz's miniscule master of understatement, exclaims, "It's lonely to be alone."

In J. D. Salinger's *Franny and Zooey*, Zooey relates to Franny the advice he received from their deceased brother Seymore and shares a profound insight with the readers: Zooey was going to appear on a panel of whiz-kids, a program which would be broadcast to a large anonymous audience which tuned in regularly with a bit of awe, and Seymore reminded Zooey to "shine your shoes for the fat lady."[3] The fact that "the fat lady" would not know if Zooey's shoes were shined or not did not matter. The fat lady was there listening, and he owed it to her to be at his best. The person habituated to being at his best probably extends his kindness into very real and sometimes crucial areas of need. Many are the fat ladies of the world.

Finally, the example of Jesus Christ in extending that personal, compassionate touch to one in need can hardly be improved upon:

"The doctors of the law and the Pharisees brought in a woman detected in adultery. Making her stand out in the

---

3. J. D. Salinger, **Franny and Zooey** (Boston: Little, Brown and Company, 1955) p. 199

middle they said to him, 'Master, this woman was caught in the very act of adultery. In the Law of Moses it was laid down that such women are to be stoned. What do you say about it?' Jesus bent down and wrote with his finger on the ground. When they continued to press their question he sat up straight and said, 'That one of you who is faultless shall throw the first stone.' Then once again he bent down and wrote on the ground. When they heard what he said, one by one they went away, the eldest first; and Jesus was left alone, with the woman still standing there. Jesus again sat up and said to the woman, 'Where are they? Has no one condemned you?' 'No one, sir,' she said. Jesus replied, 'No more do I. You may go; do not sin again.'" (John 7:53-8:11)

It is important to realize — especially since we are all more pharisaical than adulterous — that Christ was not only kind to the woman, but also to those who so self-righteously tried to condemn her. Jesus allowed them to withdraw gracefully, realizing, as T. S. Eliot so well states, "the rending pain of reenactment

Of all that you have done, and been; the shame
Of motives late revealed, and the awareness
Of things ill done to others' harm
Which once you took for exercise of virtue."[4]

---

4. Eliot, **Four Quartets**, "Little Gidding," p. 35

Social Kindness

A kindly, somewhat obese Pope who took the name John was much loved because he gave much love. He lived his words that "each man must feel in his heart the beat of his brother's heart."

We would get awfully tired of walking if all the world were paved with concrete. Grass, sand, and even mud puddles — which E. E. Cummings finds "mud-luscious"— afford variety and a certain softness on our journey through life. In order to be really aware of the hardness or softness of the earth upon which we tread we must bare our feet. "Nor does foot feel being shod,"[5] is Hopkins way of saying that man grows insensitive to the world about him when he is excessively concerned with the conventions of hurly-burly society. My point in speaking of the relative hardness or softness of surfaces, though, is this: Before we can appreciate things as they ought to be, we must deal with them as they are.

A man who remained open to a destitute and defeated people was Dr. Tom Dooley. He did not go to the Vietnamese and Laotian people pretending to have all the answers. He prayed God to "be to my virtues very kind; to my faults a little blind." He spoke to all of us in *The Night They Burned the Mountain* when he asked, "Are you willing to see that

---

5. E. E. Cummings, "In Just -" in **The American Tradition in Literature** (New York: W. W. Norton Company, 1967) p. 1572

your fellow men are just as real as you are and try to look beyond their faces into their hearts, hungry for joy? Are you willing to admit that probably the only reason for your existence is not what you are going to get out of life, but what you are going to put into it?"[6] His questions contain answers in themselves. Perhaps the most profound of these is "Are you willing to believe that love is the strongest thing in the world, stronger that hate, stronger than evil, stronger than death?"

Many have criticized the Kennedy brothers, John Lindsay, Nelson Rockefeller and others whom they believe were born with gold spoons in their mouths and must therefore apologize to society by being ostentatiously philanthropic. These men, whatever their background, have proved that they care. The tragically poor man, as I have said before, is one who has nothing *to share*. Whether a political figure investigating ways of feeding his country's poor, or a knight of the road dividing his bread with another, or a Peewee League ballplayer consoling the pitcher who just gave up a homer, kindness is the issue, Christianity is the reality.

Nothing is as unaffected, as unstudied, as a child's kindness to a child. Why? Because the child is not out to win friendship or to win esteem. He is doing what comes naturally. If a buddy skins his knee — providing that the consoler was not also the pusher — sympathy is readily offered. In the adult world tragedy often causes its witnesses to transcend

6. Thomas Dooley, M.D., **The Night They Burned the Mountain** (New York: Farrar, Straus, 1960)

motives of self-interest, and the child in each of us somehow responds. Unfortunately, though, we seem to grow less and less sensitive to tragedy. Is not the Negro's long wait for equality a tragedy? Is not the drunk's inability to make it home a tragedy? Is not the mentally ill patient left indefinitely to himself a tragedy? "Nor does foot feel being shod."

H. L. Mencken said: "The answers that most people give to human problems are neat, plausible, and wrong." If each of us responded to human problems with the same spontaneity and appropriateness that we observe in children our answers might be a little clumsier, less plausible, but more meaningful.

Kindness Transcending

Mallock has said that "character is susceptibility to motive." After what I have said about generalizations, you may be critical, but this generalization strikes me as a legitimate one. Obviously, for one's character to be "good," he must be susceptible to good motives. The whole question of determination of good and evil becomes considerably more crucial within this context. What such a question of differentiation points to, it seems to me, is one's need to transcend, to go beyond oneself for strength and wisdom. Let's consider once again the unstudied transcendence of a child.

When a child goes to his father to tell him that he has done something wrong, chances are that the father is quite aware of the transgression. What is important is not the information, but the communication; not what is unburdened, but the unburdening itself. William Peters, S.J.,[7] uses this example to show the importance of prayer in the life of each child of God. I wish merely to point out that the need the child has to go beyond himself to one to whom he feels responsible, parallels every man's search for God.

The God whom we all, consciously or unconsciously, seek the Absolute we might refer to as Yahweh, Lord, Deus, Dieu, or any other appellation, has either good motives as Creator and preserver, or bad motives. For a moment let's look at the record: God has created a universe. In that universe we "live and move and have our being" (Acts 17:28). The fact that we *are* at all is remarkable; the fact that you are you and I am me is incredible. The odds against us being us are astronomical.

Well, we are here, and we find ourselves interacting with one another, and the fact that some of us are not as nice as others, some of us are not as affluent as others, some of us are not as white (from one point of view) or as black (from another point of view), leads us to conclude that God allows a certain variety in this universe. Some of that variety (not all of it) manifests evil. Not only are there evils which we might be tempted to consider as "accidental"; there are patricides, abortions, extortions, perversions of what seems to be natural,

7. William A. M. Peters, S.J., **The Spiritual Exercises of St. Ignatius: Exposition and Interpretation** (Jersey City: The Program to Adapt the Spiritual Exercises, 1968)

or right, or good, or just. And where do we turn to find out what is really natural, right, good and just? To him who is, in Tillich's words, the real "ground of our being." Now, is he whom we refer to as God evil? Is he willing the evil we see? Or are we going against his will when we fail to do what our own best inclinations would bid us to do; when we fail to be what our own best inclinations would have us be?

Philosophers and literateurs have always been concerned with the problem of evil. The world is fraught with contradiction. The suffering of millions in the midst of plenty *should* cause a rational man to scratch his head and cast aspersions someplace.

It sometimes seems stylish to blame God for the failures of man. Is it not possible that the "something ignorant in the human heart"[8] which John Knowles isolates so skillfully in *A Separate Peace* is at the root of our imperfect universe?

When God created us, and left us free to choose him, he willed that we make other choices along our way. William T. Noon, S.J., in *Poetry and Prayer,* tells us that "in *Catcher in the Rye* Salinger depicts the evil one boy sees in himself and in those he loves. It transfixes him, and is capable of transfixing others too. It could lead to prayer."[9] Evil, in God's strange economy of things, can bring us to our knees. Wars, famines, snipings, as unexplainable as these are, and as indefensible as they seem, are permitted by God, and make

---

8. Knowles, **A Separate Peace,** p. 193
9. William T. Noon, S.J., **Poetry and Prayer** (New Brunswick: Rutgers University Press, 1967) p. 283

us very aware of the fact that this is our universe as well as his.

The problem of evil in the universe is surely that of the enigmatic force meeting the inscrutable object, the more perplexing because once one has affirmed a certain transcendence in things, both the force and the object have their elements of good. The words of the honest police chief Porfiry to the honest murderer Raskolnikov are as beautiful and as meaningful as any written by philosophers or theologians who have attempted to explain the coexistence of good and evil. Dostoevsky prefers to expose the depth of the mystery involved in the tension between good and evil:

> If you ran away you'd come back to yourself. You can't get on without us. And if I put you in prison — say you've been there a month, or two, or three — remember my word, you'll confess of yourself and perhaps to your own surprise. You won't know an hour before hand that you are coming with a confession, I am convinced that you will decide, 'to take your suffering.' You don't believe my words now, but you'll come to it of yourself. For suffering, Rodion Romanovitch, is a great thing. Never mind my having grown fat, I know all the same. Don't laugh at it, there's an idea in suffering.... No, you won't run away Rodion Romanovitch.[10]

10. Fyodor Dostoevsky, **Crime and Punishment** (New York: Bantam Books, tr. Constance Garnett, 1958) p. 397

This may seem to be the long way around, and it is, but perhaps it makes us better able to appreciate the kindness of a God who is willing to be friend enough to each of us to let us be; that is, let us be what we will. And if this is God's way of dealing with us, we can learn a great deal from him which will apply to our dealings with others.

When I have said that God lets us "be what we will," I do not mean that he leaves us entirely alone. The good father is the one who does what he can do to form his son or daughter as a responsible person, then steps aside. He does not forget his child; he is available when needed, and he wants to be needed occasionally; this is part of *his* responsibility. So it is with God.

If we would respond generously to God's will, we might find that we have greater respect for our Father's concerned transcendence, for we will have stepped outside of ourselves enough to see someone else's need to transcend.

If we are tempted to congratulate ourselves on our independence, like modern-day Ahabs chasing after our respective white whales, we may be able to say, as he did, "But e'er I break ye'll hear me crack." Yet crack he did.

CHAPTER VI

GOODNESS

She said, "will he be tried? It'll kill his mother."
So he said to her gravely, "I tried him." Then
she considered that a long time before she said, "You
forgave him." "Yes."[1]

From TOO LATE PHALAROPE
Alan Paton

Goodness is a commodity which no one will ever package. Although the scholastic dictum "Goodness is diffusive of itself" is timeless, it is also timely.

It is a sort of natural goodness, I believe, which makes the Hemingway heroes credible in their battle against *Nada*. It is the destruction of goodness which makes a tragedy. Goodness makes the world go round, in the sense that our collective desire for its preservation, despite our failure to preserve it, keeps us alive to life.

Alan Paton's novel, *Too Late the Phalarope,* and Graham Greene's *The Power and the Glory* are both graphic por-

---

1. Alan Paton, **Too Late the Phalarope** (New York: Charles Scribner's Sons, 1953) p. 19

trayals of men who could save others, but could not save themselves. I am speaking here of a psychological salvation, because I believe that God understands that the worst aspects of a human life do not add up to a stance of indifference toward him. In fact, the sensitive South African husband and the compassionate whiskey-priest are at once you, and I, and a discouraged St. Paul who articulated the human condition: "The things I would do, I cannot; and the things I would not do, those I do" (Romans 7:19).

Far from exonerating the human race from sin — for that would also incapacitate its free-will apparatus — I am increasingly aware of the dichotomy between sinfulness and sin. Goodness, it could be said, is the human tendency to be oblivious to the demands of sinfulness. I do not mean the sort of naivete which will not admit that evil exists, but the sort of realism which affirms the desirability of other human choices. It is a fairly frequent human occurence to acknowledge one's loss of innocence. I am tempted to say that one is not truly innocent until he has fallen, and perhaps fallen frequently enough to admit vulnerability and thereby to acquire an innocence which means something. I will readily admit that the innocence of a small child is beautiful, but so is the primitive splendor of a flower. Any priest or minister or doctor, and most parents, can speak of a richer beauty which has moved them deeply. It might best be labeled a "return."

In Lewis Carroll's *Alice in Wonderland* the queen awards everyone a prize. By so doing, she gives no-one anything.

Although we usually speak in terms of "observing," or "marveling at" it, goodness is no more static than any of the virtues treated in this book. If we predicate goodness of something, we are saying something about what it has given us. When we say that a person is good, we mean that he has somehow made us better. Every person has the capacity for enhancing our value, and *vice versa*. Edwin Markham spoke wisely when he insisted:

There is a destiny which makes us brothers:
None goes his way alone.
All that we send into the lives of others
Comes back into our own.[2]

Yet, what do we do with our potential creative goodness? We waste it, not by using it for evil, but by failing to use it for good. Daniel Berrigan, S.J., in what amounts to a poetic paraphrase of St. Paul's lament (Romans 7:19) points up the tragedy of omission:

Unsteady
My prayer mounts or falls. Why do I
Waste so. Want so
O make room
In the kingdom of light for lack lusters

2. Edwin Markham, "The Creed" in **Lincoln and Other Poems** (Garden City, New York: Doubleday, Doran and Company, 1935) p. 107

Among the austere and severe
For malfunctioning men
only this to their credit NO GREAT HARM DONE
Our passage writes
MAYBE on water[3]

How much better it would be if our goodness in passing
wrote WAS HERE on human hearts.

Intrinsic Goodness

By intrinsic goodness I mean man's natural tendency to
choose God or to help man. The reason that I use "or" and
not "and" is to include as a very real segment of human
society those men and women who, for all their generous
impulses, do not have the gift of faith in God.

Like Chaucerian pilgrims, we each have a tale to tell.
The rewards, even in this life, for a tale well told — that is,
a life well spent — are great. Since we are all in this life
together, even our intrinsic virtue has a social dimension. It
is fitting that "goodness does not go unrewarded." The high-
est tribute we can pay a man is our respect for what he is
doing.

The whole question of self-perfectibility, sometimes

---

3. Daniel Berrigan, S.J., "Prayer on the Six P.M. Subway," in **Love,
Love at the End,** (New York: The Macmillan Company, 1968)

erroneously seen as selfishness, has profound ramifications. Maybe today's social consciousness has had the unfortunate side-effect of undermining the individual's need to fully *be* before he can *do*.

The perfect literary example of failure to *be*, is found, I believe, in Stephen Dedalus, Joyce's young man *A Portrait of the Artist as a Young Man* and *Ulysses*. His whole being is directed toward a priesthood in art. At the end of *A Portrait* he goes "to encounter for the millionth time the reality of experience, and to forge in the smithy of my soul the un-created conscience of my race."[4] The tremendous irony is that Stephen has never paid attention to realities outside his own mind. Experience has always been read through Stephen-colored glasses, and a conscience forged in Stephen's soul will never be adequate for Ireland. Stephen's "friends"— with whom he has no deep human relationships to speak of — are trying to support Irish nationalism, or to revive the old Irish tongue, but Stephen will have none of it. He is going to be the artist-savior, and cannot see that the only artistic work created by him in either *A Portrait* or *Ulysses*, his villanelle, is the product of a solipsistic, somewhat erotic dream. Stephen wants to do the work of an artist before settling down to the task, grounded in experience, of being one.

As regards goodness, each man is good to begin with. God, our creator, produces and wills only good. It becomes a

4. James Joyce, **A Portrait of the Artist as a Young Man** (New York: The Viking Press, 1966) p. 252

case of our accepting or not accepting his will for us, his
wish that we be good, an admittedly difficult task given our
free will to disrupt his plan. Then we must help others to
realize their full potential for goodness.

Chardin unites better than any other contemporary
prophet the necessity for striving for personal perfection and
for bringing others toward Christian fulfillment. In the
Divine Milieu he states God's role:

> In each soul, God loves and partly saves
> The whole world which that soul sums up in
> an incommunicable and particular way.[5]

> My self is given to me far more than it is formed by me.
> Man, Scripture says, cannot add a cubit to his stature.
> Still less can he add a unit to the potential of his love....
> In the last resort the profound life, the fontal life, the
> newborn life, escape our grasp entirely.[6]

and our response to other men:

> To cleave to God hidden beneath the inward and out-
> ward forces which animate our being and sustain it in its
> development, is ultimately to open ourselves to, and put
> trust in, all the breaths of life. We answer to, and "com-

5. Chardin, **The Divine Milieu**, p. 60
6. **Ibid.**, p. 77

municate" with, the passivities of growth by our fidelity in action.[7]

Goodness in action, the manifesting of intrinsic goodness extrinsically, is the subject of my next reflection.

Extrinsic Goodness

Misery does not love company as much as it longs for compassion. We all have, each day, a real need to laugh, to shout, and to be silent. Perhaps we need most of all to laugh, and it is very hard to laugh alone. Simon and Garfunkel have captured the futility of lives which have become empty or meaningless in songs like "Overs," where there are no laughs left because both parties are all laughed out. The tragedy is that it happens so quickly. In "The Boxer," the fighter's life has been squandered for a pocketful of mumbles. He has been terribly lonely and can no longer live with applause alone. *He,* the person beneath the profession, tells us he is leaving, but the fighter still remains. Relationship, modern song and cinema keep trying to tell us, does make a difference. Whether it is the transforming influence of a Don Quixote in *The Man of La Mancha,* or the simple bond of understanding sought and found in *Midnight Cowboy,* it is the reality of the relationship behind the symbolic gesture which is important.

---

7. **Ibid.,** p. 138

Like a handshake which is proferred without firmness or friendship, laughs which are a sign of neither enjoyment nor mutual understanding fill empty spaces of time and are better unexpressed.

What I am trying to say is that the communication of goodness to others does not have to be a monumental thing, but rather a sincere gesture of love or concern or, at least, togetherness.

A wonderful woman in a retirement home in a tiny town in Oregon communicated more goodness to me through the slow process of syllable by syllable repetition than have countless other people whose goodness I also respect. Mrs. Mamie Peterson, who had Parkinson's Desease, could not move her tongue and form words as one would normally. It was almost lip-reading and immediate repetition of the last supposed syllable which finally enabled me to draw inteligibility from a sentence. The process would take at least five minutes for a single sentence, but I read in her patient, glowing friendly face volumes of wisdom and love of life. I never left without reading, at Mrs. Peterson's request, some Scripture and a little poetry. One time we had a great laugh together when she expressed great interest in our diverse religious backgrounds. After she had told me of her Mennonite upbringing, she said in her painfully suspenseful monosyllabic way, "We always had heard that Catholics, whom I had never met, were bastards!" I told her that some of us undoubtedly are. At any rate, we had no doubts about the legitimacy of one another as persons.

It is, of course, difficult, and not terribly rewarding, to distinguish between the personal, social, and cosmic aspects of vitues which are as nearly akin as love, kindness, and goodness. The importance of such distinction is not in pigeonholing, but in riveting our attention on realities which we have experienced, but not assimilated into our consciousness enough to make them part of our own humanness.

Goodness Diffused

In Arthur Miller's play, *Death of a Salesman,* Willie Loman emerges as the great American symbol of commonplace tragedy. Joyce had given Europe that lovable failure, Leopold Bloom; America waited for Miller's mirror, Willie Loman, to see herself by. Both character studies, interestingly, present men whose virtues and vices are divided by very thin lines. Both men have hatred for themselves and for the show they feel forced to put on. And both Willie Loman and Leopold Bloom have moments of goodness which stand in sharp contrast to their failures in the eyes of the world. Goodness is where you find it; and it can be found wherever one cares to look for it. Perhaps we should learn discernment and perceptiveness by our stumbling efforts to discern and to perceive. I am not saying that we should embark on a study of "God in all things," in the sentimental sense in which so many overly zealous and insensitive wellwishers understand the phrase. I merely say that the ordinary activities of one's day brings a man or woman into contact with countless persons and situations through which God's action in the world is made manifest. Charles Schulz gave Peanuts to the world, and in so doing he gave us yet another chance to look at ourselves, at the things we do and say and feel. And we laugh. A realization might well break over us when we see Lucy pulling the football away from Charley Brown just as he's about to kick it, that it might be "good" to save Charley from a certain amount of frustration by letting him actually kick it now and then. But we know, and Schulz constantly reminds us by often repeating the tragedy that we, in our all-too-human way, more often than not pull the football away from those with whom we deal.

There is more than a little truth to the words Pope penned in his "Essay on Man:"

Placed on this isthmus of a middle state,
A being darkly wise and rudely great —
Created half to rise and half to fall,
Great lord of all things, yet a prey to all;
Sole judge of truth, in endless error hurled —
The glory, jest and riddle of the world![8]

---

8. Alexander Pope, "Essay on Man" Epistle II, in **Alexander Pope: Selected Poetry and Prose** (New York: Holt, Rinehart and Winston, 1965) pp. 138-9

The fact that man is good — whether because of his weakness or in spite of it — remains the mystery which makes all extrinsic goodness more remarkable. Somehow, in some wonderful, crazy way we have experience of those who answer Macbeth's sad question:

> Canst thou not minister to a mind diseased,
> Pluck from the memory a rooted sorrow,
> Raze out the written troubles of the brain,
> And, with some sweet oblivious antidote,
> Cleanse the foul bosom of that perilous stuff
> Which weighs upon the heart? (*Macbeth*: V, III, 40-45)

with a clear, joyful, unequivocal "Yes." It is only when each man fails to be who he can be for others that life becomes "A tale told by an idiot, full of sound and fury, signifying nothing." (*Macbeth*: V, v, 27-28)

CHAPTER VII

FIDELITY

"Faith consecrates the world; fidelity communicates with it."
Teilhard de Chardin in THE DIVINE MILIEU

A great deal has been said and sung about communication in recent years. What is so often misunderstood is that communication is a means, not an end. What does it mean to "communicate" with the world? We might attempt here to analyze what fidelity means in concrete terms, and how fidelity can be said to communicate with the world as we know it.

Fidelity or faithfulness certainly can be discussed from the point of view of covenant as is exemplified in all of the Old Testament writings. It might also be considered as a virtue of feudal society, in which a knight was faithful to his liege in a way that would be incomprehensible to either a modern employee or employer. As valid as these approaches might be, there is again an archetype for fidelity found in the relationships among the members of a loving family.

Fidelity is one of those realities which embraces far more than the avoidance of its opposite. It is a positive covenant of acceptance of one another as one another, and for the sake of one another. Fidelity is not merely non-adultery or non-promiscuity or non-complaint. It is a faithfulness to oneself — to one's manhood or womanhood — and to one's world. It is, in the final analysis, a fidelity to life, with all its obligations. This sort of fidelity transcends faithfulness to a vocation, or to an avocation, to any given task. William Butler Yeats states quite succinctly the fate which awaits one who chooses to perfect a work in which he is involved to the detriment of life-obligations. "The Choice" begins:

> The intellect of man is forced to choose
> Perfection of the life, or of the work,
> And if it take the second must refuse
> A heavenly mansion, raging in the dark.[1]

It is of himself that he speaks, for Yeats was convinced that as a poet he had made the choice of "the work." Whether or not Yeats is correct is another matter. The fact is that there is truth in his statement if one becomes so involved with a part of reality that his vision of life is impaired.

Fidelity, as we have seen, can best be observed in married couples whose total commitment to each other is so great that they act as one, and thereby communicate the reality of their love to the world they live in. When such a marriage is blessed with children, the children themselves are living

---

1. Yeats, **Selected Poems and Two Plays of William Butler Yeats,** p. 132

testimony to the father and mother's fidelity to each other and to life. The next best example of fidelity is seen in friendship, and of all the friendships captured by contemporary litterateurs, that of Santiago and Manolin, the old man and the young boy in *The Old Man and the Sea,* is the most beautifully unaffected.

Manolin's concern for the well-being of the old man and Santiago's affection for the boy are obvious from the beginning. Each is a support to the other. The boy realizes that he can learn much from such a courageous friend and knowledgeable fisherman. In the course of the story the old man struggles with the marlin he has come to love, and the sharks he undeniably hates. Santiago believes that it is fidelity to his life's work as a fisherman which primarily accounts for his fight to live. Later, though, he makes a significant statement: "...everything kills everything else in some way. Fishing kills me exactly as it keeps me alive. The boy keeps me alive, he thought. I must not deceive myself too much."[2] In other words, he, and we, deceive ourselves if we think that anything — including love of God — keeps us going, apart from the love and friendship and fidelity experienced in our relationships with other persons. It is easy to deceive ourselves in this regard, but the picture becomes clear only when we begin to consider fidelity as a kind of communication with our world.

2. Ernest Hemingway, **The Old Man and the Sea** (New York: Charles Scribner's Sons, 1952) p. 106

We do not exist in a vacuum; our responsibilities are not to an amorphous blob called humanity, but to individuals who happen to be our parents, husbands, wives, children, friends, and countless persons whom we have met, or will meet, or will never meet, but to whom we owe our fidelity.

Cardinal Newman paraphrasing Marcus Aurelius once said, "Fear not that your life shall come to an end, but rather that it shall never have a beginning." If it is fidelity through which we most deeply communicate with our world, then each of us must begin to be faithful if we are to begin to live fully, and to have something meaningful to communicate.

St. Paul's letter to the Philippians seems to me to describe the results of fidelity in Christian life:

> If then our common life in Christ yields anything to stir the heart, any loving consolation, any sharing of the Spirit, any warmth of affection or compassion, fill up my cup of happiness by thinking and feeling alike, with the same love for one another, the same turn of mind, and a common care for unity.
>
> (Phil. 2:1-3)

Fidelity to One's Self

"Lovers and madmen," says Shakespeare in *A Midsummer Night's Dream,* "have such seething brains, / Such shaping fantasies, that apprehend / More than cool reason ever comprehends" (MND: V, i, 4-6). When we are truly loving, or a little crazy, we do seem to apprehend a great deal. Perhaps we must be a bit mad before we can truly love. It is certain that whatever our level of apprehension, we have the hardest time seeing ourselves, seeing our unique love or our unique madness. At least part of the problem is that we are really unfaithful to ourselves. We are least solicitous about our own ability to love, and our own need to be a little mad.

We can always look at others looking at us, as did Eliot's J. Alfred Prufrock:

And I have known the eyes already, known them all —
The eyes that fix you in a formulated phrase,
And when I am formulated, sprawling on a pin,
when I am pinned and wriggling on a wall,
Then how should I begin
To spit out all the butt-ends of my days and ways?
And how should I presume?[3]

but it is infinitely more profitable to look directly at ourselves. I do not mean that we should get hung up on what we might have been, or what we should have done. We should assess our potentialities, and, if we have failed to do what we might have, we should begin to be faithful to that one God-created and cared for self. Polonius' sententious words to his son in

3. T. S. Eliot, "The Lovesong of J. Alfred Prufrock" in **Selected Poems** (London: Faber & Faber, Ltd., 1961) p. 13

Hamlet are, if correctly understood, valid, for all their sententiousness:

> ...to thine own self be true,
> And it must follow, as the night the day,
> Thou canst not then be false to any man.

We also have a real human need to communicate with ourselves. Edward Albee has ruthlessly torn the veils from the many games and escapes that keep us isolated from ourselves and from others. *Who's Afraid of Virginia Wolf* exemplifies the sort of "exorcism" which can only be wrought when basic love and fidelity exist between persons. When the fantasy-world of Martha has at last been shattered, when she is made to accept the reality of her inability to bear a son, the following dialogue ensues:

Martha: (a long silence between them) Did you...did you...have to?
George: Yes.
Martha: It was...? You had to?
George: Yes.
Martha: I don't know.
George: It was...time.
Martha: Was it?
George: Yes.[4]

---

4. Edward Albee, **Who's Afraid of Virginia Woolf?** (New York: Atheneum, 1963) p. 240

It is such a terribly hard lesson for us to learn that we must be faithful to ourselves in order to accept reality; and, if we are in the position to do so, faithful to those we love in order to help dispel their illusions — even if this means shattering their illusions about us. Fidelity hurts. Again, witness Charley Brown. He asks Linus, "What would you do if you felt that no one liked you?" Linus candidly replies: "I'd try to look at myself objectively and see what I could do to improve." Charley, and we, respond: "I hate that answer."[5]

The world of athletics offers numerous examples of men and women who have made terrific sacrifices because of fidelity to an ideal. Jack Olsen's fine article in the July 1, 1968 *Sports Illustrated* on "The Black Athlete" is particularly moving in its treatment of Don Smith of Iowa State and Elvin Hayes of Houston, two of the most talented college basketball stars in many years. Both men had run with tough neighborhood gangs; both realized that poor boys who had no books in their houses, bad backgrounds, and the need for attention, chose "the only way they could get any attention." With increasing awareness that they could become great basketball players with study and practice, they began doing just that. It is important to note the correlation between the fidelity that people showed to men like these, and the fidelity which they had to their own ideals.

John F. Kennedy's book, *Profiles in Courage,* supplies still

---

5. Charles Schulz, 1968 Peanuts Calender: Determined Productions, Inc., San Franciso, California

more food for thought, as does his own life. He, his brother Bob, Martin Luther King Jr., Carl Stokes, mayor of Cleveland, and countless other courageous people, all men who have followed ideals without counting the cost, are real monuments to the type of courageous fidelity which signifies the Spirit of God.

Why is it that the mother changing diapers, the janitor who refuses to sweep the dirt under a rug, the father who takes time to give and to receive in his family, the faithful nurse, doctor, priest, and farmer force us to look at ourselves? Fidelity, it seems, begins with self, proceeds to others, and activates a world.

Fidelity to Others

"I truly prefer emeralds, Tweetums, but we could have made it on green glass." Carol Channing's statement to Julie Andrews in *Thoroughly Modern Milly*, serves as a fitting springboard for our discussion of applied fidelity. The remark in the context of the movie referred to the relationship between Muffy (Carol Channing), and her multimillionaire husband. He had given her an emerald brooch, but it was the giving and not the gift that was important.

Fidelity is a dynamic gift-relationship, a continual process of offering one's self and being receptive of another. Obviously, fidelity is the most telling manifestation of the love, and manifestations are always signs of interiorized attitudes. There is, as Shakespeare noted, "a tide in the affairs of men," and the ebb and flow of love might be said to be affected by the moon of fidelity, which is always there, even when the sun of circumstance makes it hard to perceive.

We want so much, so fast, it seems. We want things for ourselves. We want things for others. Quite naturally, we want others to be what we would have them be. Most of our breaches in fidelity occur in this area. How does one let go of another, and yet remain faithful — and perhaps be more faithful because of letting go?

If I may return to the analogy above — first disclaiming any familiarity with things astronomical — I wonder if the moon's seeming vigilance over the sea and the sea's seeming wilfulness and independence might offer a hint toward a Christian resolution of the difficult problem of proper detachment.

A young man and a young woman, after a period of growth toward each other, celebrate together the beautiful sacrament of matrimony. In due course, the young woman becomes a mother. If the husband finds his wife difficult to live with after a time — and I do not refer to problems which would warrant separation — he must ask himself how honest he is, and how honest he should be in light of the tremendous commitment he has undertaken. Fidelity does not mean that life together is a bed of roses. The title of Hanna Greene's excellent study of schizophrenia, *I Never Promised You a*

Rose Garden, comes to mind. Perhaps we do promise one another rose gardens in one sense, but roses have thorns. Whatever metaphor you prefer for the reality of a given commitment, the fidelity required is inextricable from the covenant entered upon.

An anecdote in a letter from Chuck Schmitz, a Jesuit missionary in Zambia, expresses better than I could the privelege of procreation. When he asked a 10 year old Zambian boy, "How did God show man that he loved him even after original sin?"— fully expecting the conventional answer that "He sent his Son as a Redeemer"— the boy replied: "He told Adam and Eve that they should increase and multiply." The profundity of the answer stunned the boy's teacher, and me. Who has ever fathomed God's love for us?

In marriage, the primary commitment is to one's spouse, but there is also a commitment to God, to one's children, family, friends and community. To renege on a commitment which has been made with understanding is to break down the fiber of sacramentality, insofar as every reflection of God's presence is a sacrament, and every failure to accept God's action in our lives tends to make the easy way out the acceptable way out.

There is in the world today a marked tendency toward deepness or shallowness in commitment. In other words, people are more involved and less involved, and the people "more or less" involved in responsible living are beginning to weaken and renege. When a society's various commitments break down, it is the youngsters who cannot understand what is unintelligible or irrational — and their scars are deep.

Commitment, like ice cream, melts if not consumed. When consumed by fidelity, it strengthens the consumer and spares someone a mess.

Fidelity to a World of Others

The life of faith and a life of fidelity differ considerably. The words of Chardin which began this chapter offer a clue to the differentiation. "Faith consecrates the world." The person who lives a life of faith, who believes in God's presence, "makes holy" the realities he experiences and influences. The person who has fidelity communicates his faith to the world.

The December 15, 1967 *Time* magazine essay "On Being an American Parent" quoted educator Clark Kerr as advising parents to, "Spend time, not money." The advice is sound, whether one is speaking of parenthood, national domestic programs, or international aid. The parent or public official who pampers his charges with material goods but fails to attend to personal needs, personally administered, does not exhibit Christian fidelity or responsibility.

It is very difficult for any of us to feel great love for or fidelity to people we do not know, people who live in Cairo or Cebu or New Guinea. It is almost impossible to reside in the security of a defined relationship. However, we have responsibilities as humans to humanity.

As critical as some people may be of certain policies of missionaries or of Peacé Corps workers, we must admit that the people involved in these programs are witnessing to the fidelity of the few to the many.

For all of the talk about the generation gap, we must never allow a "humanity gap" to develop. The only way that we will effectively close the gaps which exist between nations and between cultures is to bring our technological know-how and our energy to those who will accept the help to help themselves. When we force ourselves, or our conception of government, on others we defeat our purpose, because we succeed in creating others in our own image.

Dag Hammarskjold, probably the best authority on world fraternity, left us a number of wise observations, including a statement which, as expectation and reality converge, expresses doubt and hope. If a man who knew so much about the many could dare to strive even as he wondered, can we refuse to get involved?

> I am being driven forward
> Into an unknown land:
> The pass grows steeper,
> The air colder and sharper.
> A wind from my unknown goal
> Stirs the strings of expectation.

Still the question:
Shall I ever get there?
There where life resounds,
A clear, pure note in the silence.[6]

In William Faulkner's *The Sound and the Fury*, optimism and pessimism stand in stark contrast, and I believe that they might shed some light on our consideration of the universe at large. Quentin tells us that his father sees that man is "the sum of his misfortunes," and later, that "men are just accumulations, dolls, stuffed with sawdust swept up from the trash-heaps where all previous dolls had been thrown away."[7] Dilsey, on the other hand, is moved by the words of the Negro preacher: "Den, lo! Yes, Breddren, Whut I see? Whut I see, O sinner? I sees de resurrection and de light; sees de meek Jesus sayin Dey kilt Me dat ye shall live again; I died dat dem whus seen en believes shall never die." Dilsey, we are told, "made no sound, her face did not quiver as the tears took their sunken and devious course, walking with her head up, making no effort to dry them away even."[8]

I don't know if most of us are capable of the quiet dignity of a Dilsey, but we may be able to affirm, as she did, the beauty of the Christian mystery over the sort of determinism

6. Dag Hammerskjold, **Markings** (New York: Alfred A. Knopf, Inc., 1964) p. 5

7. Faulkner, **The Sound of the Fury**, p. 218

8. **Ibid.**, pp. 370-371

which makes no efforts to help others "live again" because a pre-determined life has no apparent meaning.

If we are to have fidelity toward a world of other men, an attitude of living faith in our own resilience, a desire to "spend time, not money," in whatever ways we can within the context of our personal responsibilities, then we need to see, in some way, "de resurrection and de light." We need to sense God's presence to us in our time of need.

CHAPTER VIII

GENTLENESS

Meanwhile
Watch the indolent butterfly playing on the tall flower
in the yard
And think about the sun's going down
It always does you know.[1]
Rod McKuen in
LISTEN TO THE WARM

In a culture which scorns softness, gentleness is also unsung. It is true that there seems to be an upsurge of effeminacy, and continual incense raised to the great god Luxury, yet gentleness is not in evidence. I conclude that gentleness is really a virtue for the strong and for the detached.

I believe that there is an amazingly accurate analogue between the plight of the under-achiever in our society and the death of gentleness, or *gentilesse* as Geoffrey Chaucer termed it. The student who has given up, whether or not he

---

1. Rod McKuen, **Listen to the Warm** (New York: Random House, Inc., 1967) p. 16

has taken the logical step and "dropped out" of the ratrace of achievers, is not necessarily lazy or stupid or hostile. He, for a number of reasons, has ceased to be motivated. Let's look at the ordinary classroom situation in a typical American high school. Let's observe the stresses on a boy who did not pay attention in the early part of a given year, and who has consequently found himself too far behind to catch up. He is not exactly thrilled by his inability to excel.

First of all, he has found himself in an atmosphere of evaluation — by his teacher, and by his peers. Secondly, that evaluation has resulted in criticism. Further, since his teacher is a symbol of authority, that teacher must seem to know all there is to know about the subject which he, the student, is failing. And, finally, the rigidity of the teacher-student structure makes it impossible for the boy to articulate his frustrations or what might be creative observations. I am not exonerating the student from blame; I am asking whether his condemnation to the ghetto of underachievement might be at least partly the fault of our system of judgmental education.

The wise teacher will try to get away from categorical instruction, memorization of material for which there is no discernible application, and from a value structure which will impress on the student his own absolute stupidity. A teacher does not have to be wishy-washy or naively client-centered to do this. He or she must be firm, but gentle. After all, education is not, or should not be process whereby a teacher leads a student to his insights, but rather one where the student's own insights are valued. No one educates anyone else; the teacher facilitates the student's education, brings the material before him in, hopefully, an interesting manner, and then gets the hell out of the way. In the words of Dr. Earl Kelley, "It is what the person *sees* that is enabling or disabling."[2] Sometimes our society categorizes as dropouts those who see a great deal more than we are willing to admit.

The increase in cases involving people who have dried up or dropped out of life seems to me to find a correlation in the failure of families, churches and educators to be firm but gentle. It may be that one cannot be the latter if he refuses to be the former.

Rod Steiger's moving performance in the film *The Pawnbroker* captured for us the difficulty encountered by a man so numbed by the tragedies around him that he cannot be receptive to those who have obvious need for a gentle word or a kind deed. Only the death of a young man who respected the pawnbroker (Rod Steiger) enough to protect him could bring compassion and sympathy to the surface, a little late.

In *Two Women* Sophia Loren beautifully portrayed the strong and gentle mother of a young girl to whom a degree of hope had to be restored after both mother and daughter had been cruelly raped by a band of Turks leaving Italy after the war. It is admittedly easier to see what is required of us when

---

2. Earl C. Kelley, "The Fully Functioning Self" in **Perceiving, Behaving, Becoming** (Washington, D.C.: Association for Supervision and Curriculum Development, 1962) p. 9

tragedy occurs. We have become more sensitive to the day-to-day tragedies which require our gentleness and our strength.

We laugh at the blindness of a myopic Mr. McGoo, the little man who has such a hard time identifying what he sees before him; but there is no virtue in mistaking water hydrants for baby buggies, and less in mistaking unmotivated or disillusioned persons for bad risks or total losses.

The Gentle Man

Carpe diem was the expression that the Roman poet Horace used in encouraging his peers to take advantage of the present moment. The literal translation of his words is "pluck the day," something which American society might well heed. There seems to be an innate procrastination in the fibre of our lives. We always have an excuse for not beginning. Our history of deferral begins early. Wait till grade school, wait till you're a teenager, wait till you're a senior, wait till you're 21, wait till you're married, wait till you're established, wait till middle age, wait till retirement — wait long enough and there will be no present moments left to pluck. Many scientists and ecologists tell us that there is enough breathable oxygen on the earth's surface to sustain thirty years of human life, at best. Still we react tokenistically. We consider building a B-1 long range bomber fleet at the estimated limit cost of twenty-five billion dollars. It will probably take thirty years to determine that the finished planes are obsolete. Meanwhile pollution perdures. Let's apply this sort of putting off to the business of gentleness.

Gerard Manley speaks to himself on himself when he says:

My own heart let me have more pity on; let
Me live to my sad self hereafter kind,
Charitable; not live this tormented mind
With this tormented mind tormenting yet.[3]

We have already discussed patience with self, and touched on both charity and kindness, virtues which have much in common with gentleness. Gentleness is more concerned with the way in which we approach that self of ours which is always becoming. What often happens, I believe, is that we actually put off being gentle in our own regard, just as we tend to put off exteriorizing our desires to constructively help others.

The three-hour CBS special on The Cities, presented in June, 1968, dramatically brought before the American public the huge problems involved in increased suburbanization with the concomitant trend toward detachment from the problems left behind in the big city ghetto. It struck me that there should be a dramatic way to bring to our consciousness the very similar problems we ignore as we stretch toward what

---

3. Hopkins, "My own heart let me have more pity on . . ." p. 66

we feel is self-fulfillment by wrongly motivated involvement. The reason that we try to escape our cities and escape ourselves is that we fear violence from that part of our society and that part of ourselves which we have not taken the time to control. It is very much a question of gentleness to ourselves which is required by both situations. We are, that is, in a situation which requires that we accept our responsibilities to ourselves and to our world before we can begin to consider moving away from our problems.

Too often, I believe, all of us reason thus to ourselves: I may be avoiding confrontation with myself in the area of my own unique spirituality or my own unique sexuality, and so forth — *but* I can continue to get involved in my job or with my family, and save myself the unpleasantness of commitment to God or to myself or to my friends. Similarly, the average white, middle-class American says to himself: I may be avoiding coming to grips with the deterioration of this city where I work, but no longer wish to live, but I can move to the suburbs where there is little pollution and no race problem, and help my local suburban Chamber of Commerce make a healthy, happy community for my family.

A real practice of the virtue of gentleness begins with the real me and extends outward to the real needs of the whole community of men of which I am a small part.

The lovable old fisherman, Santiago, in Hemingway's *The Old Man and the Sea* is an archetypical gentleman in the sense that he never seeks to escape from the responsibilities imposed by the harsh realities of bad times and hard work. He continues to fish *correctly* because he owes it to himself and to his profession to do so. When it came to catching "the truly big fish," after eighty-four days of bad luck, he thought, "Now is no time to think of baseball . . . Now is the time to think of one thing. That which I was born for."[4]

I have often reflected that it is highly probable that the greatest idealists are also the greatest realists.

Gentleness to Other Men

Why is the King a Fink? I doubt if even the comic-strip's "Wizard of Id" has asked himself what it is about his pint-sized sovereign that makes him so unpopular with the masses. I think that it has something to do with the king's insensitivity to the real needs of the Idians. A recent episode chronicling the king's barnstorming carriage ride through his realm depicted the king telling his subjects that "If you elect me I'll put this town on the map!" When they applauded, he turned to the royal mapmaker and said "Put it on the map." Applause should not be the criterion for implementation of new measures — even such trivial innovations as the king's. Necessity is still the mother of invention. And inventiveness, or creativity, is an underlying factor in our discussion of so many virtues in

---

4. Hemingway, **The Old Man and the Sea**, p. 40

this book. One may be gentle by nature, but gentleness — like any other Christian virtue — is, in its application, creative in two senses.

First of all, gentleness re-creates its object. The objects of our gentleness are not necessarily persons, but I can't imagine a person considering himself the least bit Christian whose gentleness extends only to animals. So let's stick with persons. When we are sensitive to someone's needs or even likes, and gently help or encourage that person, he becomes more fully himself, and is re-created in a sense, if only by the fact that there is comfort in the security that someone cares what he needs or likes.

Secondly, gentleness re-creates the gentle person. One of the great mysteries of Christianity seems to me to be the reciprocity which operates when one is trying to practice Christianity. In the Roman Catholic Mass there was, before the changes in the liturgy, a beautiful prayer taken from Psalm 115 which captures the paradox of Christian living:

> What shall I return to the Lord for all that he has given me? I will take the chalice of salvation and call on the name of the Lord, singing His praise. (Psalm 115)

The point of the paradox — that my proper return to the Lord is my acceptance of salvation through him — is that it is by re-creation that we are re-created. The McKuen poem which began this chapter appealed to me precisely because it conveys a sense of gentleness without killing us with explicitness.

There is in nature a sort of built-in gentleness and a sort of disruptive violence which parallel's our human moods. Strangely, the cavorting of "indolent butterflies" or the convulsing of the wind-torn sea can remind us of God. Why do we have such a hard time seeing the presence of God in one who is deranged as well as in one who is calm and self-possessed?

Gentleness to other men is largely an attitude or habit which even those whom we have discussed as "kind" may not possess. It seems to me that a little added attentiveness characterizes the gentle person. Of all the virtues discussed thus far in this book, gentleness is the one most easily written off by the people who least understand and most cling to "manliness." The greatest and strongest men I know have the capacity to attend to the little hints each of us drop about our needs and aspirations, and they gently guide us where we need to go. Each of us know's down deep, what Wallace Stevens meant when he said, "I needed a place to go in my own direction," a place from which he might look down and recognize his "unique and solitary home."[5]

Christ's example would obviously be helpful here, but you and I have known other Christs, perhaps a large number of them, who by their gentle awareness have made our lives more liveable, made it easier for us to be Christians in deed as well as in name. The Royal Air Force pilot, John G. McGee

5. Wallace Stevens, "The Poem that Took the Place of a Mountain" in **The Collected Poems of Wallace Stevens** (New York: Alfred Knopf, Inc., 1964) p. 512

Jr., reminisced about his experiences flying "up, up the long, delirious, burning blue," where "with silent uplift mind I trod the untrespassed sanctity of space; put out my hand and touched the face of God."[6] We need never leave the earth to have the same experience.

Gentleness in the World

That Gentleman of La Mancha, Don Quixote, spoke the following words on his deathbed to Sancho Panza: "Pardon me, friend, that I caused you to appear mad, like me, making you fall into the same sort of error as myself, the belief that there were, and still are, knights errant in the world." Finally, after countless events which would have disillusioned a man of smaller heart, he learned that realism must attend generous impulse if it is to be generosity at all. His final words were: "let us go gently, gentlemen, for there are no birds this year in last year's nests. I was mad, but I am sane now." His epitaph candidly affirms that he "had the luck, with much ado, to live a fool, and yet die wise."[7]

"The luck to live a fool" — maybe we all need to be foolish enough to extricate ourselves from the conventions of our milieu and attain the madman's over-view. Maybe we all suffer from a realism which is really pragmatism, or expediency,

---

6. John G. McGee, Jr., "High Flight" in **Prose and Poetry of America** (Syracuse, New York: The L. W. Singer Company, Inc., 1955) p. 163

7. Miquel de Cervantes Saavedra, **Don Quixote** (Baltimore: Penguin Books, 1967) p. 937

or complacency. Maybe if we attacked a few more windmills we would slay a few more dragons.

A paradox which I have discussed at several points in this book is worthy of still more emphasis. To be productive of good — whether the good is made manifest by gentleness or fidelity or whatever — we *must* be constructive. But, more than likely, we must be a bit destructive too. There is nothing better for the soul, I maintain, than a little healthy iconoclasm.

To bring about gentleness in the world is going to require salesmanship. If our product, Christianity, is worth selling, then we should not be ashamed to sell it. Taking my lead from a famous sales axiom which goes: "Sell the sizzle and not the steak,"[8] I say, "Don't sell Christianity, sell community."

I do not believe in reducing all men to the same common denominator, creating a community of goods, or establishing a welfare state. In fact, I am rather violently opposed to all of these on the basis that true human dignity and personal initiative, particularly each man's right to become what he can become, would not only be compromised, but usurped.

What I do believe in, and this is admittedly and necessarily idealistic, is corporate effort by mankind to alleviate the suffering and injustice which has arisen as a result of that very initiative, a privilege which, if abused, does violence to the rights of those who may wish to exercise their own initia-

---

8. Elmer Wheeler, **Tested Salesmanship II** (Elmer Wheeler Sales Training Institute, 1950) Chapter on Sizzlemanship

tive, but have not, or could not. Those of us who have swept a certain amount of dirt under our respective rugs by saying that if someone has failed to make as much a go of life as we have, it must be his own damn fault, might learn a great deal from people who have missed educational opportunities because they had to work at an early age in order to help keep food on the family table. Some day, and soon, we must, as human beings, own up to the fact that we have failed in being human in a fundamental way that requires us to become ourselves by extending our aspirations beyond ourselves.

As we listen to report after report of our aid to Israel, Russia's aid to Egypt, our aid to Jordan which loses no love over Israel, and our aid to Southeast Asia which loses no love over us, we are tempted to say that plans for world peace are hopelessly unfounded. And we are right, so long as our pocketbooks dictate to our consciences, and not the other way around. Oh, I know, we are exporting freedom, and have never ceased supporting motherhood, but how many of us believe that either freedom or motherhood mean as much to Americans as we would like to have others think? "What is honored in a country," observed Aristotle, "is cultivated there." Enough said.

Gentleness is attitudinal. We must choose to extend gentleness to a world which is, because it chooses to be, violent. We do not begin to effect a transformation by preaching gentleness. We might make a start if we, as individuals, as a nation, as a people — sons of one God — practice honesty and nail down the rugs.

CHAPTER IX

SELF-CONTROL

*And this is my prayer, that your love may grow
richer and richer in knowledge and insight of
every kind and may teach you by experience
what things are most worthwhile.*
Phillippians 1:9

The effort we make to analyze our choices is not always
repaid, because we are all human enough to make most of
our choices for no discernible reason at all. Experience,
though, is not only a hard teacher, but a fairly reliable one.
While we do not always make good choices, we certainly do
tend to choose what we think is good. Insight, like love, and
self-control, is a grace, a gift we often wish we could present
to ourselves.

Why control self at all? For the sake of our own viable
selfhood, and especially for the sake of others. Lack of self-
discipline may not mean the end of the world, but it may force
another's world of possibilities to a close. Dissipation through
drugs or sex or drink or selfishness is not always clearly culpa-
ble, but it always brings pain to family and friends.

A great deal of debate has attended the legislation for control of firearms. Statistics seem incontrovertible: Deaths by guns will decrease if registration is enforced. The important thing to note is that few (if any) reasonable persons have advocated that guns be abolished. Control means accepting what I have and controlling its use. As television commercials have reminded us, there is "a tiger in the tank" of each of us. The best thing we can do is keep the cap on.

The self-possessed, self-controlled individual is he who can look the world in the eye with the full knowledge that as little love as he has to give is so much more than he can afford to waste. When we waste love, we waste ourselves. There is a grim parallel between Shakespeare's insight into time's revenge and our cloudy apprehension of love's paradox: "I wasted time, now time doth waste me."

I chose the quotation from St. Paul's letter to the Philippians as an introduction to the grace of self-control for two reasons. First of all, because Paul's prayer asked that their love grow richer and, secondly, that that love grow richer in insight, in the perception of what is going on inside as one chooses, by experience, the things that are most worthwhile.

The excerpt is admittedly loaded, and I think we can reflect profitably upon the role that love of self and insight into one's choices play in our efforts to maintain self-control.

The stress throughout this book may seem to have been upon externalization of Christian attitudes. I have not wished to play down the necessity for self-actualization based on self-realization. One of my favorite songs has simply conceived and profoundly meaningful lyrics: "What the world needs now is love, sweet love; it's the only thing that there's just too little of."[1] If there is a dearth of concretized loving, and there is, then it probably reflects a dearth of self-love in each unique individual. If we are to control our drives and appetites and habits which develop naturally, yet limit our effectiveness in loving by fragmenting our attempts, then we must love ourselves enough to say "no" when our giving in to an impulse might jeopardize a future, constructive "yes." I know, it seems like the ice cubes in a pitcher either come out all at once or not at all. It is the dilemma of the luke-warm lemonade or the ruined table cloth. In either event, love of self might dictate whether we enjoy the more cooling drink or the less embarrassing manner of pouring.

Literature and life tend to focus upon those persons who exhibit a lack of self-control. For every Rhett Butler there are a hundred Thomas Sutpens and Tom Joneses.

This may not seem to be the most appropriate time to speak of death, but there is, I feel, something about a person's controlled, peaceful facing of death which is an index to his or her posture toward life.

All of us have experience of the dying process. Each day we let go of more and more in order to take hold of something else. Two friends of mine, one a relative, the other a mother of boys whom I know well, accepted death by cancer in a remarkably cheerful way. Neither friend ever brought up the subject of his or her personal suffering, but when we conversed it was obvious to me that both had chosen not to fight death when the moment of taking hold of a new life drew near. My cousin did not want to leave life and his loving wife any more than the mother wished to separate herself from her husband and children. Both realized, however, that their forty or fifty years had been full and happy, even if difficulties asserted themselves periodically in order to affirm human contingency.

Their peaceful deaths did not sadden me too much. Their love of life and control of themselves filled me with admiration and love of human goodness.

Self-Controlled

Marianne Moore defines poetry as "imaginary gardens with real toads in them."[2] With all deference to poetry and to Miss Moore, we must now talk about real toads in real gardens — our own. There is a lot to be said for demythologizing; when it comes to our own unique selves, we must do a little deromanticizing too. It would be nice if everything about us were dramatic, but, really, we just aren't that interesting.

---

2. Marianne Moore, "Poetry" in **The Penguin Book of Modern American Verse** (London: Penguin Books, Ltd., 1954) p. 115

We love the sensational, but the hour-by-hour, minute-by-minute work toward achievement of self-control has little glamour about it.

Kamala, the wise and beautiful courtesan in Hermann Hesse's *Siddhartha,* gives the young Indian boy advice which will mean much to him when he renounces the pleasures and success of the world to become a Buddhist monk: "One can beg, buy, be presented with, and find love in the streets, but it can never be stolen. You have misunderstood."[3]

Major Scobie in Graham Greene's *The Heart of the Matter* had also misunderstood. Because he mistook pity for love, and effectively loved no one, I believe that he ended up in a state of very forgivable but unfortunate self-pity which God, though Scobie doubted it, could and would forgive. Self-control is not a prerequisite for salvation. God's mercy transcends our mistaken fits and starts, but it certainly helps us to help others and thus fulfill our purpose in life if we can do some of the work ourselves.

In the matter of loving, no amount of well-wishing, no amount of trading will help us to love and be loved. We must be fully ourselves and, consequently, most lovable, and fully in control of our potential for loving and, consequently, most capable of love. If we mistake emotionality or infatuation for love, we will never be self-possessed.

---

3. Hermann Hesse, **Siddhartha** (New York: New Directions, 1951) p. 58

There is an abiding, stable quality about self-control. It is not just temperance, nor detachment, nor reserve. It is somehow analogous to the hub of a wheel, or the core of a good apple, and very like the vigil light which Captain Charles Ryder, in Evelyn Waugh's *Brideshead Revisited*, observed burning in the old chapel at Brideshead, "something none of us thought about at the time: a small, red flame — a beaten-copper lamp of deplorable design, relit before the beaten-copper doors of a tabernacle; the flame which the old knights saw from their tombs, which they saw put out; that flame burns again for other soldiers, far from home, farther, in heart, than Acre or Jerusalem."[4]

Our self-control, as hard as it is for us to gain, exists, ultimately, for others as well as for ourselves. It too is a gift of the spirit, a sign of God present to us, a sign of our presence to others.

Control is so much more than a negativistic self-denial. It is the free, vibrant choice of a man who is fully a man, or a woman who is fully a woman, to live a rich life with a clear knowledge of himself or herself. The existential fact of personal weakness or inadequacy in no way diminishes the self-control which such a person makes himself free to exercise. As Linus, my favorite Peanuts character, so simply and knowledgeably affirms, "No use kidding myself; without this blanket I'd crack like a piece of old bamboo."[5]

---

4. Evelyn Waugh, **Brideshed Revisited** (Boston: Little, Brown & Co., 1946) p. 350

A little security is not the same as a little escape .One takes reality into consideration; the other flees from it.

Self-Controlled for Others

Estragon and Vladimir are waiting for Godot. Vladimir belittles Estragon's "blaming on his boots the faults of his feet,"[6] and both wonder exactly where it is that they are to wait for Godot, who is to offer a prayer for them. They discuss various things they might do, but decide that it is better to wait. Vladimir says ironically, "Let's wait till we know exactly how we stand." At the end of Becket's two-act tragicomedy a boy tells Vladimir that Mr. Godot does nothing, yet when Estragon awakes from a nap, the two continue waiting. They can wait, at least, together.

Becket's anti-heroes are very much like us. They never really listen to each other, and never do much to take their destinies in their own hands. Every time they say "Let's go," they stand still. There is a certain security in waiting, in not forcing issues to a close. But there is little virtue here. Self-control, for the sake of others, implies galvanization. The longer we wait for Godot, the less chance there is that he will come. The better prepared we are to *be* Godot for others, the better able we will be to find him ourselves.

5. Schulz, Peanuts Calender, 1968

6. Samuel Beckett, **Waiting for Godot** (New York: Grove Press, 1954) p. 8

Why was it that Othello loved "not wisely but too well?" Because he was not sufficiently in control of himself to admit that Desdemona might really love him too much to hurt him. She was so much in control that she could forgive what she could not understand.

We all have trouble, as Quentin Compson did in Faulkner's *The Sound and the Fury,* accepting "ordered certitudes, long divorced from reality." By coming at some realities which have profound religious significance, I have not wanted to offer easy answers where there are none. Especially in the area of self-control, each man is pretty much his own judge. We are each our best selves or something less than that. Perhaps we actually are our best selves while *seeming* to be somewhere on the "dud scale" between Charley Brown and Iago— the latter really doing his best at being evil; the former doing his best, period— and failing.

We've got to remember that all reality has its supernatural dimension, a sort of direction which we must become increasingly sensitive to, both for our own sake and for the sake of others. Chardin, commenting on the Scripture phrase, "All things work together unto good for those who love God," says, "That is the fact which dominates all explanation and all discussion." And it is.

Self-control or any other struggle is meaningless apart from love of God. Asceticism for the sake of asceticism is more absurd than waiting for a million Godots.

A World of Selves: Freedom and Constraint

When I said that becoming Godot is better than waiting for him to come, I didn't intend sacrilege. Godot is most probably God to Becket. The fact that his God demands patience in requiring the willing suspension of unbelief, doesn't alter the issue. Pozzo and Lucky, the two rather unattractive characters who enter the waiting world, and who significantly become blind and deaf respectively — *are* Godot too. I'm sure that what the playwright had in mind is the scriptural assurance that "whoever loves the least of these, loves me." God is where you find him.

How does all of this relate to self-control on the cosmic scale? We are in control in order to be free. We are free precisely in order that we might be others Christs to a world which is largely blind and deaf to the light and word of God continually manifesting himself. When Vladimir and Estragon have a chance to help Pozzo and Lucky, they hesitate, until Vladimir finally realizes that the cries for help were not just idle petition, but "to all mankind they were addressed, those cries for help still ringing in our ears! But at this place, at this moment of time, all mankind is us, whether we like it or not. Let us make the most of it before it is too late."[7] If God, then, is in a sense the savior and the saved, and no one need wait for manifestations of God which are more patently divine, how, in the words of Yeats, do you "tell the dancer

7. **Ibid.**, p. 51

from the dance"?[8] Discernment is the best justification, I believe, for constraint; and the *sine qua non* of freedom. I will treat discernment in depth in the concluding chapter.

Paul Morel, in D. H. Lawrence's *Sons and Lovers,* is a young man who has been possessively treated by his mother to the extent that he could not give of himself enough to marry Marian, who really loved him. Self-control can hardly be achieved without a certain emancipation from those who must know when to withdraw their protection. The mature man is he who is able to know his own unique self-value enough to communicate that value to others, without relinquishing his selfhood in the bargain.

True shared love does, in a way, immortalize the partners. A man and woman, each exercising self-control, find themselves most free when they are bound.

John Donne, speaking as man to God, poetically pinpointed this reality in "Batter My Heart": "That I may rise and stand, o'erthrow me."[9] Freedom plus constraint is almost a working definition of self-control, and the ramifications of this grace are cosmic. The world of today is challenged, not overcome, by food shortages, violence, confusion, amorality and considerable immorality. The evils of world-wide racism, coercion, and deprivation of human dignity are the chief areas

---

8. Yeats, "Among School Children" in **Selected Poems and Two Plays of William Butler Yeats,** p. 117

9. John Donne, "Batter my Heart" in **John Donness Poetry** (New York: W. W. Norton and Company, 1966) p. 86

in which enlightened Christians can and must promote fraternity, freedom, and ennoblement. Talk is cheap; action is costly. We need to pay the price. John Courtney Murray, S. J., in *We Hold These Truths* said that "man lives both his personal and his social life always more or less close to the brink of barbarism, threatened . . . by the decadence of moral corruption, and the political chaos of tyranny. Society is rescued from chaos only by a few men, not by the many."[10] Nothing would be wrong with being barbarous, were we not part of the civilized world. Since we claim civility, let's really be civil and help the few become the many, a society of free yet constrained human beings, creatively paying the price for world freedom and world constraint.

A song I quoted earlier, "What the world needs now is love, sweet love," continues, "No, not just for some, but for everyone."

---

10. John Courtney Murray, S.J., **We Hold These Truths** (New York: Sheed and Ward, 1960) p. 13

CONCLUSIONS

*"Be not too hasty," said Imlac, "to trust
or to admire the teachers of morality:
they discourse like angels, but they live like men."*
Samuel Johnson
THE HISTORY OF RASSELAS

Self-styled teachers of morality, do, thank God, live like men. Johnson's Imlac might have done better to counsel the young Rasselas to beware of teachers who felt themselves exempt from the exigencies of the human condition. Morality, if it is to have any relevance for men, must be founded upon a critical evaluation of man's day-to-day trysts with a world much loved by a very real God.

I have never really decided whether beginnings are more important than conclusions, or *vice versa,* but the conclusion of this particular book is especially important inasmuch as it represents a beginning. The graces of the Spirit enumerated in the past chapters do not exist in any abstract, textbook sense. They are contextual; they are wedded to realities which you and I have experienced or will experience. Although T. S. Eliot warns us that "human kind/ Cannot bear very much reality," I will try to make real application of what we have discussed, but "the times they are a-changin'" — and Eliot, again, bids us

"See, how they vanish,/
The faces and places, with the self which, as it could,
  loved them,/
To become renewed, transfigured, in another pattern."[1]

In the Introduction, I spoke quite a bit about prayer, and
the fact that social consciousness leads to self-confrontation,
and personal inadequacies frequently force us to place ourselves, as we are, in God's presence. The chapters of this book,
based as they were on the nine manifestations of the Spirit of
God, have been concrete instances of God's presence to us
intersecting with our day-by-day experience. The suffering,
redeeming, glorifying and glorified Christ is very much present to the world today. The signs of his continual coming
among us are Love, Joy, Peace, Patience, Kindness, Goodness, Fidelity, Gentleness, and Self-Control.

The most creative of contemporary literary figures, Joyce
Carey's lovable and maddening lover and madman, the artist
Gulley Jimson in *The Horse's Mouth,* makes some observations on his brand of Christianity which may be closer to the
ideal than any of us have, till now, been willing to admit:

Look at Christianity. Just a lot of floating seeds to start
with, all sorts of seeds. It was a long time before one of
them grew into a tree big enough to kill the rest and keep
the rain off. And it's only when the tree has been cut into

---

1. Eliot, **Four Quartets**, p. 4

planks and built into a house and the house has got pretty old and about fifty generations of ordinary lumpheads who don't know a work of art from a public convenience, have been knocking nails in the kitchen beams to hang hams on, and screwing hooks in the walls for whips and guns and photographs and calendars and measuring the children on the window frames and chopping out a new cupboard under the stairs to keep the cheese and murdering their wives in the back room and burying them under the cellar flags, that it begins even to feel like a real religion. And when the whole place is full of dry rot and ghosts and old bones and the shelves are breaking down with old wormy books that no one could read if they tried, and the attic floors are bulging through the servants' ceilings with old trunks and top-boots and gasoliers and dressmaker's dummies and ball frocks and dolls-houses and pony saddles and blunderbusses and parrot cages and uniforms and love letters and jugs without handles and bridal pots decorated with forget-me-nots and a piece out at the bottom, that it grows into a real old faith, a masterpiece which people can really get something out of, each for himself. And then, of course, everybody keeps on saying that it ought to be pulled down at once, because it's an insanitary nuisance.[2]

Granted, Gulley's statement of the case for a pulsating

---

2. Joyce Cary, **The Horses's Mouth** (New York: Harper and Row The Perennial Library, 1965) pp. 193-194

Christianity is a bit strong, but the truth of the matter is faith in God is lived out in a world of men; the community of Christians re-creates a world to be lived in.

The advent of Jesus Christ in the world meant that the Word — the expression of all that the Father is and intends for us to be — was made flesh. Love became man. Joy became man, and so forth. All other virtues are ancillary to these, for, as St. Paul pointed out, "There is no law dealing with such things as these" (Galatians 5:23) and counsels us: "If a man should do something wrong, my brothers, on a sudden impulse, you who are endowed with the Spirit must set him right again very gently. Look to yourself, each one of you: you may be tempted too. Help one another to carry these heavy loads, and in this way you will fulfill the law of Christ" (Galatians 6:1-2). It is in helping one another that we will fulfill the law, not in scrupulously observing a set of axioms or imperatives.

I have tried to draw reflections of life as it is from my own experience, and the experiences of friends, from contemporary litterateurs, modern song-writers, and a few other diversified sources in order to provide a few "hints and guesses" about the direction which I feel contemporary creative Christianity must take. I am not advocating the disbanding of churches as we know them; rather, I think that priests and pastors who are alive to the pulse of life about them can do a great deal to direct the generous impulses of those whom they have been fortunate enough to find under their charge. All Christians must begin to share in priestly transformation of our world.

When I mention Christ's coming at a particular time and place in history, it is with the greatest respect for the historical ramifications of the Incarnation. God's ways, if there are still those who doubt it, are certainly not our ways. It is his way to show us new ways, better ways to extend in time and in space the creative incarnations of Christ to every human being.

When we speak of manifestations of the Spirit, we necessarily speak of the difficulties involved in discerning the Spirit. There are in literature a number of discerners, persons who observe life and human behavior, then try to judge how they can best live fulfilled human lives in which they do not have to compromise on principle. Three such men of discernment are Pietro Spina, the revolutionary in Igazio Silone's *Bread and Wine*, Ishmael, narrator of Melville's classic, *Moby Dick*, and Nick Carroway, the narrator of Fitzgerald's *The Great Gatsby*.

Spina, seeing the decadence and usurpation of liberty under the emerging Fascist dictatorship of Italy, places himself on the line, discerning both the need for his sacrifice and the results of his choice. He, ironically disquised as a priest, becomes the most Christian of men in a land teeming with the corrupt clergymen of that time.

Ishmael goes to sea to find out about life. He has faults, yet he generally recovers equilibrium. After initially rash-judging Queequeg, the savage who proves to be "George Washington, cannibalistically developed," Ishmael befriends the huge harpooner, despite society's rumblings. Later, after becoming so emotionally involved in Ahab's mad quest that he admits he has "looked too long into the fire" to be reliable, Ishmael gains balance and openness from his experiences, and is the only member of the Pequod's crew who can grasp the implications of Ahab's attempt to absolutize evil, and then put a harpoon in it. Even if Ahab "has his humanities," Ishmael recognizes that the captain has sold out to an impossible dream.

Carraway comes home from the East coast wanting the world to "stand at moral attention forever" after seeing the corruption which attends the social status-seeking and irrational violence of sophisticated Easterners. Although Jay Gatsby himself was a prime example of a person caught up in the materialistic American Dream, Carraway discerned that Gatsby was oddly innocent of the corruption which floated in his wake. Nick also realized that to Gatsby all natural beauty and goodness seemed grotesque once he had opted to live for material value alone: ". . . he must have felt that he had lost the old warm world, paid a high price for living too long with a single dream. He must have looked up at an unfamiliar sky through frightening leaves and shivered as he found what a grotesque thing a rose is and how raw the sunlight was upon the scarcely created grass."[3]

---

3. F. Scott Fitzgerald, **The Great Gatsby** (New York: Charles Scribner's Sons, 1925) p. 162

All of these discerners, and we who must open our eyes to the world as it is, have the difficult task of trimming our own lamps enough to grasp the implications of an incarnational presence operative in our lives, and lasting values which are ours for the choosing. As Dr. Reilly asserts to Celia in T. S. Eliot's *The Cocktail Party*, both conventional living and living with an element of risk are viable options. "Neither way is better. Both ways are necessary." *But,* "It is also necessary to make a choice between them."[4]

There is something to be said for a candle's value in providing light and heat even as it consumes itself, but there is no percentage in burning ourselves out for a goal which is not worthy of our energy, our life, or our love.

One final example of discernment of value which I have found particularly striking is that of the mode of operation at Morning Star Boys' Ranch in Spokane, Washington. Father Joe Weitensteiner and his staff provide a real atmosphere for responsible growth for the thirty boys who share the work and the play, the success and the failure of one another as they collectively grow toward self value. The discernment necessary to guide such an operation between the extremes of rigor and reward seems to me to represent an apprehension of value in the unique individuals who are amateurs still in coping with the ambiguity of living, and experts at being boys, The *esprite corps* and loyalty to one

4. T. S. Eliot, **The Cocktail Party**, (New York: Harcourt, Brace and Company, 1950) p. 141

another exhibited by the Ranch boys attests to the success of discipline in a context of Christian co-responsibility.

We are weak and shortsighted; we must expect to find as Christ's; that our joy has failed to reflect his joy; that our peace is not as salutary as his peace. But that doesn't mean we should give up. Contrary to certain of the tenets of American pragmatism, the effort is more important than the results. A community of believers believing or a community of workers working will never accomplish as much as a community of believers working because they believe in those for whom they work and in him on whose account they work.

This has been a book on praying in the here and now. It calls for faith; it calls for creativity; it calls for a sense of wonder at the world of possibilities. It calls for the sort of discernment in the hurly-burly now which Hopkins had when he found God present even in the catastrophe he commemorated in "The Wreck of the Deutschland":

> Thou mastering me
> God! giver of breath and bread;
> World's strand, sway of the sea;
> Lord of living and dead;
> Thou has bound bones and veins in me, fastened me flesh,
> And after it almost unmade, what with dread,
> Thy doing: and dost thou touch me afresh?[5]

It calls for the maturity to become children at the request of

---

5. Hopkins, "The Wreck of the Deutchland" p. 11

the God-man who reminds us daily through our experiences that "unless you turn round and become like children, you will never enter the kingdom of Heaven," and "whoever receives one such child in my name receives me" (Matthew 18:3). Finally, this book calls for the type of commitment to daily discernment and Christian compassion I believe that T. S. Eliot sensed, and tried so hard to articulate, when he wrote:

> . . . to apprehend
> The point of intersection of the timeless
> With time, is an occupation for the saint —
> No occupation either, but something given
> And taken, in a lifetime's death in love,
> Ardour and selflessness and self-surrender.
> For most of us, there is only the unattended
> Moment, the moment in and out of time,
> The distraction fit, lost in a shaft of sunlight,
> The wild thyme unseen, or the winter lightning
> Or the waterfall, or music heard so deeply
> That it is not heard at all, but you are the music
> While the music lasts. These are only hints and guesses,
> Hints followed by guesses; and the rest
> Is prayer, observance, discipline, thought and action.
> The hint half guessed, the gift half understood,
>   is Incarnation.[6]

Prayer is incarnation; love, joy, peace, patience, kindness,

---

6. Eliot, "The Dry Salvages" p. 27

goodness, gentleness, fidelity and self-control are the concretizations of our prayer in our lives. Our lives as Christians raise ever-old, ever-new music to the world; and I pray with you that we will "be the music while the music lasts."

Creativity is the greatest part of living. You and I are fulfilled in direct proportion to our creative activity. I do not mean that we have to father large families, although actual fatherhood is a beautiful, concrete form of creating. What we must do, as creative Christians, is father forth timely plans for helping each other to live full, happy, Christian lives. The creative energy, I feel, is provided by the thrust of a life of prayer — prayer, that is, as I have attempted to define it in this book: daily awareness of God's presence to you and to me as it made manifest to us in the persons and events we encounter. We are who we are; God knows that. We can become most fully who we are when we allow other persons to impinge upon our unique worlds, and when we bring to the world something of ourselves. With Eliot, I have tried to cast this discussion of moment-to-moment incarnating of the Spirit as "hints and guesses" because there is much mystery involved in each of our lives, and much that is up to the action of God. The fact that "the hint half-guessed, the gift half-understood is Incarnation" merely confirms the words of St. Paul that "the Spirit comes to the aid of our weakness. We do not even know how we ought to pray, but through our inarticulate groans the Spirit himself is pleading for us, and God who searches our inmost being knows what the Spirit means, because he pleads for God's own people in God's own way" (Romans 8:26-28).

God's own way is to incarnate his Word and his presence; and our prayer, our concrete rendering to God his due and receiving him in the person of other men, is our creative continuance of Incarnation.